Expert Women Who Speak...

Speak Out!

Volume 2

As Canadian women who speak professionally, we dedicate
this book to the countless number of women in the world
who are not allowed to use their voices nor speak their truth.

Introduction

Welcome to a unique and exciting project created by some of the most unique and exciting women in Canada! We are women who are professional speakers, and who come together with one vision and intention: to provide you with a book filled with the essence of our knowledge, skills, and wisdom. This is a book that you can use to provide you with new information and approaches to help you with the broad range of work, personal, and interpersonal challenges that you face daily in this rapidly

Editors: K. Glover Scott and A. Alfano

moving world. As women, we are constantly growing and changing. You'll find inspiration and direction to assist you in becoming all you can be, so you can live your life from the essence of who you really are.

The women who have contributed to this book are leaders in Canada. You have heard some of their names before, and some will be new to you. You may have experienced a keynote presentation by one of these awesome women, or attended a seminar that has made an impact upon your life. As women who speak, we have chosen a profession wherein we know we can make a difference in the world, and in the lives of the people and organizations with which we work each and every day.

To be a professional speaker is not an easy road to choose. One must possess focus, tenacity, drive, foresight, and a lot of heart. One must have a 'thick skin' to be able to stay motivated and excited by her/his work when the engagements are limited, and to have limitless energy when times are so busy that there does not seem to be enough hours in the day. The speaking profession is also one where a professional needs to be constantly reinventing her/himself, to change with the times and the needs of her/his audience. Its also a profession where the work 'behind the scenes' – such as marketing, research, accounting and writing – dictates that we wear many different hats in one day, each and every day.

Who, then, is better suited to this profession than a woman? Women are consummate multi-taskers who know how to go the extra mile. We are passionate about the needs of others, and will ensure that they are met to the best of our abilities. We are experts at making connections, forming relationships, and changing course at the drop of a hat. As communicators and listeners, we have been leaders since the beginning of time. All of our remarkable qualities and abilities can shine in this profession of speaking. And, the authors of this book are paid professionals who express the best of who they are daily in their work.

What also makes us unique as authors of *Expert Women Who Speak, Speak Out!* is that we are members of the Canadian Association of Professional Speakers. Our not-for-profit national organization has the mandate to develop 'experts who speak' through mutual support and education. Our organization also promotes Canadian speakers both nationally and internationally. Visit our informative website at http://www.canadianspeakers.org.

It is amazing how many different topics, and how much information, can be found within the covers of one book! Yet, the topics covered fall in to three distinct categories. **Empowerment**, or finding your uniqueness and strength in life, and living fully from it, is one area. Another is **Balance**, which is, at times like searching for the Holy Grail in our lives as women today. And the third area focuses on **Success** – both personally, and in the world of business and work. With such a diverse range of information you can use this book as a source of guidance and help, whenever you are feeling stuck or challenged in your life. Also, visit the websites of the authors (found with their biographies in this book) for further information, insights and learning.

We would like to thank Sandy Ross of Wordsworth and the staff of Double Q Printing. As the editors, we are thrilled to be bringing this group of women's voices together on one platform! We hope that you experience our passion, pride and professionalism on your journey of learning.

-Kathy Glover Scott M.S.W. and Adele Alfano, Editors

Table of Contents

Words of Wisdom by Canadian Women from Our Past

Few women are enrolled among the makers of Canada. Yet, in all save the earliest years, they have formed nearly half the population and have done almost half the work. But, historians and businessmen tell us little of the part they have played. The women's stage was not set in the limelight, but the firelight.
-*Isabel Skeleton, traveler in the backwoods, 1924*

Women who set a low value on themselves make life hard for all women.
-*Nellie McClung, suffragist, author and MP*

All my life, I have recommended that one must ask questions, take a position, and act upon it.
-*Therese Casgrain, Quebec suffragist and politician*

I believe that never was a country better adapted to produce a great race of women than this Canada of ours, nor a race of women better adapted a great country.
-*Emily Ferguson Murphy, First Woman Magistrate in the British Empire*

Eight Keys for Champion Success

By: Penny & Vicky Vilagos
World Champions and Olympic Medalists
Vilagos International

How to become a champion in your field.

Champions are made, not born. This, we know from experience. When we were in elementary school, our teacher approached us one day and said, *"Penny and Vicky, you've been chosen, along with four other kids, to miss music class and go to remedial gym."* Obviously, we were not natural athletes, and certainly not born champions. In fact, we were so poorly coordinated, we couldn't even catch a ball!

Each year, when our gym teacher announced, *"Next week we'll be doing the Canada Fitness Test"*, we cringed. We dreaded the six-event physical fitness challenge that was part of the school gym program. It included the 50-yard dash, the shuttle run, the broad jump, sit-ups, the flexed arm hang, and the 300-yard run. Most kids achieved at least the bronze level; many reached silver or gold. All we ever got was a participation certificate.

You are a champion when you live up to your true potential.

Thankfully, we didn't stop trying to find sports and activities that we might enjoy. We then discovered synchronized swimming. It seemed to be a perfect blend of everything we were good at, and we were soon hooked! We had discovered our passion, and we followed our hearts. With the help of a supportive coaching team, we competed for 21 years, winning many championships at the national and international levels. Each victory boosted our motivation, and each setback forced us to reach down deep and grow stronger.

We have found that the lessons we learned as athletes apply to all aspects of our lives. By sharing our stories with you, we hope that you will find parallels with your own aspirations, and that you, too, will become a champion in your field.

What is a Champion?

First, let's define *champion*. We believe that you are a champion when you live up to your true potential. You develop the talent you were born with, concentrating your efforts on achieving a goal that will make you happy. You continually pursue excellence. As a champion, you also know that life is not all about winning and losing. You use your talent to make a difference in the lives of others.

You may be a seasoned business leader, or just starting out. You may work in a service industry, or volunteer your time to make your community a better place in which to live. You may be a mother, choosing to spend your time with your children until they are older. Or, you may be planning to forge a new path after retiring from your first career. Whatever your situation, to become a champion, consciously determine the path that is right for you, define success for yourself, and then follow your heart's desire with passion and single-minded resolve.

You may have found the field that is right for you, or you may still be looking. Figuring out the right path may not be a simple task, so take some quiet time away from everyday demands to reflect on your purpose. Asking yourself the following questions will get your ideas flowing, and use the space below to write down your new awareness:

1. What did you love doing as a child?

2. What type of work would you do, even if you were not paid?

3. Fast-forward 20 years in your mind. As you look back, is there anything you wish you had done?

_____

_____

_____

_____

_____

Identify your strengths and weaknesses, without being too hard on yourself. The key is to make the most of your strengths. Define your potential and your own measures of success as they relate to the personal, family, and professional aspects of your life. Determine your ideal balance of these, then spread your wings and soar! Form visual images of success in your mind, and feel the emotions. Create a scrapbook with images that represent your success – call it your 'dream book.' It will serve as a beacon.

> *"What one great thing would you dare to dream if you knew you could not fail?"*
> - *Brian Tracy, author and speaker*

Stop and think about this. Do you have any self-limiting beliefs holding you back? You may have trouble imagining yourself actually achieving your dream. But, the wonderful truth is, each of us has the power within to become a champion. The first – and critical – step is choosing to exercise that power.

The eight letters of *CHAMPION* can pinpoint the character traits common to all champions – traits you can nurture and develop in yourself. As you read, keep a notebook handy to capture your thoughts … then put your plan into action!

Courage

Champions have courage. They move beyond their fear of failure to pursue their dreams, and they know that preparation is the key to performing well under stress.

During the first 14 years of our swimming career, we had achieved all of our objectives except one: we failed to make it to the Olympics – twice. We retired from the sport in 1985, and each pursued business careers. Then, five years later, while watching a regional synchro competition, we were struck with the desire to give it one more try.

We were afraid to announce our comeback in case we did not succeed. However, we were more afraid of not trying, and then spending the rest of our lives wondering what might have been. We decided to go for it, and to be proud of ourselves just for giving it our all. We focused on our dream, and how we felt, not on what anyone else might think. Part of the reward would be discovering whether we could reach our maximum potential.

Fear of failure is one of the most significant obstacles that you may face. Don't let it stop you from pursuing the life of your dreams. As you prepare to follow your heart and become a champion in your field, learn to define failure in a new way. Failure provides you with lessons, stepping-stones on the way to your eventual success.

If you are ever overcome with fear, think of one action you can take, no matter how small. Then, visualize positive outcomes, and go for it. From time to time, you may be pushed to your limits. Each time you stretch yourself beyond your comfort zone, you will discover strength you didn't know you had.

As athletes, we also had to learn to compete under pressure. After a full year's work, our results were determined by how well we swam a single four-minute routine on a given day. Imagine how we felt when people said, *"Millions of people will be watching you when you compete in Barcelona!"* We managed our anxiety through positive self-talk, which we had practiced over the years. Although we always had butterflies in our stomachs right before competing, we were able to concentrate and feel confident in our ability to perform well.

Fortunately, most people do not have to face stress of Olympic proportions. However, from time to time, you will face a critical moment when you need to perform at your best. It may be a job interview, a final exam, an important presentation, or a sales call. Preparation is key. The more prepared you are, the more confident you will feel. *Have the courage to overcome your fear of failure.* Dare to believe in your dream, and pursue it with conviction, energy, and passion.

Habits

Champions have effective daily habits. They hone their skills to produce optimal performance, and know that the cumulative effect of small constructive actions performed repeatedly will contribute significantly to their success.

We strove for excellence in our duet routine. We had to achieve identical timing, height, and angles in the water, all while executing technically difficult moves with near-perfect form. On each beat of music, we needed to get two or three details just right. That added up to more than 500 thoughts or corrections in four minutes! Developing the right habits was the only way we could attain the level of performance we required. We repeated each move hundreds of times, making the corrections automatic. We also reviewed every detail of the choreography early on to ensure that bad habits did not become ingrained.

We are all creatures of habit. However, we are often unaware of the little things we do. Becoming conscious of your 'automatic pilot' is the first step toward eliminating unproductive habits, and building new ones that will help you succeed. Start by paying close attention to your habits relating to job skills, as well as those that affect how smoothly your day runs or your overall productivity. Determine whether there are any changes you could make that would contribute to your success.

Be clear about why you need to change a habit. Outline the long-term benefits. Without a strong drive for change, chances are, you will go back to doing things the old way. See if you can find someone else who can support you as you commit to maintaining your new habit.

Here is an example to demonstrate how a small change can have a powerful impact. Many people enjoy relaxing in front of the television in the evening. If you read daily for just 30 minutes instead of watching that extra sitcom, it adds up to over 180 hours per year! Think of how many books you could enjoy in that time. Books can be a source of relaxation, inspiration, or ongoing learning. Applying your new knowledge can help advance your career. If you are a parent, you will also be setting a good example for your children.

Another habit that many of us have developed is putting things off until tomorrow. Consciously work to overcome procrastination. Develop a 'do-it-now' attitude, and deal with problems while they are still small. The payoff for you will be almost immediate, both in terms of increased productivity and peace of mind.

Daily good habits produce a current to help you move closer to your goal, whereas bad habits can make you feel as though you're swimming upstream. Strive to *develop winning habits.*

Attitude

> Champions have a positive attitude. They look at what can be achieved, and what can be learned from setbacks along the way. This constructive attitude affects their emotions... and their results.

Faced with the daunting challenge of competing on the world stage in only two years, our team knew there was no time to waste. Our four coaches said, *"The only way to get time on our side is to make every minute of every practice count."*

We put a rule in place that gave us a competitive edge: we agreed to maintain a *can-do* attitude every day. We reminded each other to stick to this rule, and it helped us form a cohesive team. The quality of our practices was higher than ever before, and we set our sights on a measurable improvement every single week. When problems arose, we were tempted to say, *"It's just not fair."* It was hard to train, work full time, and pay for our competitions in Europe. We even felt that complaining was justified when none of our funding requests came through. But, we knew we had nothing to gain by blaming others. Instead, we pulled together and kept our spirits high. Despite all the hard work, we enjoyed our sport and we had fun. At times, we laughed so hard with our head coach, Julie Sauvé, that we ran out of air and sank to the bottom of the pool. Julie used positive words when giving us corrections. We trained our minds to focus on 'what to do' rather than 'what not to do'.

A positive attitude is contagious! When you adopt a positive attitude, people want to be around you, and they want to help you. Focus on opportunities and solutions rather than setbacks and problems. Keep things in perspective and smile. Say to yourself: *"I can do it"* and *"That was much better than yesterday."* Continually aim to improve, and remember to pat yourself on the back for each accomplishment along the way. Celebrate your successes, and develop an attitude of gratitude!

Take control of your thoughts. They will influence your emotions which, in turn, will affect your response to events. A positive response produces improved results. Make the most of your opportunities – *decide to adopt a positive attitude.*

Mission

> Champions have a mission – a clear sense of purpose. Establishing clear objectives based on that mission helps them to maintain focus and stay on track.

We knew exactly what we wanted, but we didn't know how to get there, so we turned to our coaches for help. They each had a different specialty, but our team shared a common sense of purpose. Together, our coaches developed a detailed two-year practice and competition plan. They set concrete objectives for all aspects of our training program, including speed swimming, flexibility, weight training, compulsory figures, and duet routine.

Each time we dove into the pool or worked out in the weight room, we knew what we had to accomplish. Our short-term objectives were to get back in shape, and develop our strength. We also had to learn the new synchronized swimming techniques that had evolved during our five-year hiatus. As a medium-term challenge, Julie boldly registered us for an international meet in Germany in November 1990 – only seven months after our comeback! Our long-term objectives were to win the Canadian Olympic trials in April 1992, and then, deliver the performance of our lives at the 1992 Olympics.

Once you have determined what your dream is, take the time to develop your own personal mission statement. It will anchor your dream in reality, and provide you with a greater sense of meaning. Let your mission reflect the type of balance that you desire in your life.

Next, define your short, medium, and long-term objectives, and set target completion dates. Anticipate foreseeable obstacles so you can keep surprises to a minimum. If you need help developing or achieving your plan, ask a mentor to assist you.

Short-term objectives are critical. They help you to take the first step, which is often the most difficult one. They give you something specific and manageable to shoot for. As you experience incremental success, your confidence will increase and you will feel able to stretch toward your medium-term objectives. These provide you with a renewed source of motivation, and serve as checkpoints along the way. Assess your progress and determine whether any adjustments are required. Your long-term objectives serve as a beacon, and help you focus on what is important.

Fewer than five percent of adults actually write down their personal mission statement and objectives. Those who do are far more likely to succeed. Do yourself a favour and invest in your success – take the time to write them down. You'll gain a greater sense of urgency, clarity, and focus. And remember, it's okay to make changes along the way. Once it's down on paper, be sure to *review your personal mission statement every day.*

Passion

> **Champions live their lives with passion. An intense flame burning within provides them with the passion and energy they need to follow their heart's desire.**

We had been startled by the realization that our Olympic dream was still alive while watching that competition in 1990. It was as if the old flame had re-ignited deep within us. In a flash, we had made a decision with our hearts: *"We want to swim in Barcelona!"* Our coaches were as passionate as we were. Our hearts raced and our eyes lit up with excitement as we discussed our Olympic pursuit. Once we had made the decision to go for it, we felt more alive and raring to go at the start of each day. The sacrifices we had to make did not seem as painful, since it was for such a worthwhile cause. We were thrilled to be back in training and doing what we loved.

As you look to your future, dream big dreams. We are not suggesting that you aim for the Olympics – focus on what matters most to you. Your ambition could be to earn a promotion of the level of Senior Management, spearhead a campaign for your favourite charity, or to complete further studies in your field.

To make your mission really come alive, follow your heart, visualize your success, and feel your emotions. When you love what you do, it doesn't feel like work. In addition, people around you will get a boost from your positive energy.

Take the time to think about your work – is your heart really in it? If you do not find it engaging, but are unable to make a change now due to responsibilities and obligations, make the experience more fulfilling by focusing on the aspects that you do enjoy. Then develop a longer-term plan to enable you to live the life of your dreams. Passion keeps you going when the going gets tough. Logic is not enough. Harness the energy that comes from your heart, and *follow your dream with passion.*

Integrity

> **Champions have *integrity*. They live in accordance with their values and high moral standards, and develop strong and productive relationships based on trust.**

In synchro, total duet scores are calculated by adding 50% of the routine score to 50% of the compulsory figures score. During the figures competition, each swimmer completes six highly technical moves individually, one in front of each panel of judges. All swimmers must wear identical black bathing suits and white bathing caps to promote anonymity. For duets, it is essential that *both* swimmers earn high marks in figures, since their two scores are averaged.

Over the years, several people have said to us, *"Hey, you guys could switch, and have the twin who is stronger in a given figure do it twice!"* It certainly would have been easy to do, and we are confident that no one would have been able to tell. But we never considered doing it, even if it might have meant the difference between winning and losing. Had we won under such circumstances, we would certainly *not* have been champions. As it is, we are able to look back upon our achievements with a wonderful sense of pride.

These days, we often hear stories of corruption – in sports, in business, and in religious institutions. It would be easy to become cynical. Many people are feeling the squeeze from downsizing, and are being asked to do more with less. It may be tempting for them to compromise their ethics and cut corners, but it doesn't pay. A sterling reputation takes time to build, but can be destroyed in an instant.

> **Integrity is crucial to successful leadership. People will not follow someone they don't trust. As you build trust through your actions, you get better results. And as a respected leader, you benefit from long-term loyalty.**

Each day that you live up to your word, and treat others with respect, you will develop stronger relationships based on trust. Abide by the spirit – not just the letter – of your agreements. As you help others succeed, others, in turn, will help you. When you are true to yourself, and take responsibility, you can take pride in your work. Demonstrate your character as you live in accordance with your values and principles. *Always do what you know is right,* and you will stand out as a shining example of integrity.

Organization

> Champions have strong *organization*.
> They focus on doing what is most
> important first, giving themselves a sense
> of control, and making their efforts more
> productive.

Although it was a tremendous challenge to work full-time, and then train five hours a day, our priorities were crystal clear. This helped to ensure that our time was focused on activities that would contribute to achieving our dream. We didn't have the luxury of doing fun stuff before important stuff; there was no time for procrastination. We just got things done.

We became experts at multi-tasking, reading industry reports late at night while sitting in the splits, and focusing on creative problem solving while swimming laps. However, when something required our full attention, we turned all our energy towards it. We gained a sense of control, and enjoyed a tremendous sense of accomplishment. It was energizing and personally satisfying.

As you pursue your endeavours, make the best possible use of your time. Analyze what is really important, and what is simply busy work. Get in the habit of asking yourself: *"How is this going to help me achieve my goals?"* Make effective use of 10 minutes here and 20 minutes there. You'll be amazed at what you can accomplish.

Achieving balance is an ongoing struggle. To realize your dream, it may be necessary (in the short term) to devote most of your energy to one area of your life. If that pulls you away from your family, try to find ways to involve them, and help them see the big picture. And, be sure to set aside some time to recharge your batteries. Strive to achieve your desired balance over the long-term.

When doing something important, focus your attention on the task at hand. It doesn't help to worry about your family while you are at work, or to worry about work while you are with your family. Stay in the present – you'll be less stressed and more productive.

In addition to making good use of your time, organizing your physical space will help boost your productivity and sense of inner peace. Frankly, this has not been one of our key strengths, but we're still working on it. After all, self-improvement is an ongoing process!

Get in the habit of making a list of your completed tasks at the end of each day, and planning your priorities for the following day. You will accomplish more, and have more reasons to celebrate, as you *focus on the most important things.*

Never Give Up

> **Champions never give up. They believe in themselves and keep going when faced with adversity. They have self-discipline, and are determined to achieve their goals.**

The year after coming out of retirement, we headed off to compete at the 1991 Canadian National Synchro Championships. We swam our duet routine to the best of our ability. When the marks were announced, we froze on the spot. We had placed second. This was not part of our plan!

Now, we would be underdogs going into 1992, and everyone thought we would quit. People said, *"I can't believe you're going to train five hours a day – after a full workday – for another whole year without knowing if you can win the Olympic trials!"* But, we were determined. We believed we could do it. And we'd promised ourselves, 'Nothing is going to stop us this time.' In April 1992, we won the Olympic trials, and went on to live our Olympic dream.

Don't expect to reach your goals without having to overcome some adversity. Believe in yourself. Be resolute in your commitment to your mission. Adjust your path if you need to, but don't give up. A setback is only temporary… unless you quit!

If you do find yourself wanting to quit, sit quietly and reflect. Close your eyes, and visualize the fulfillment of your dream. Remember how important it is to you. Trust yourself. Review your accomplishments to date, and let it sink in that with each step you take, you are one step closer to achieving your goal. You have the self-discipline within you to do what it takes. Show that you are willing to pay the price. Becoming a champion requires a lot of hard work. Only those who persevere ultimately realize their potential. *So believe in yourself, and don't give up.*

Remember that you hold the key to your own success. To be a *CHAMPION*, you have only to decide to:

Courage   Have the courage to overcome your fear of failure.

Habits   Develop winning habits.

Attitude   Decide to adopt a positive attitude.

Mission   Review your personal mission statement every day.

Passion   Follow your dream with passion.

Integrity   Always do what you know is right.

Organization   Focus on the most important things.

Never give up   Believe in yourself and don't give up.

Follow your dream, harness the power within you, and become a champion in your field. You will achieve tremendous satisfaction as you progress toward achieving your true potential.

Take charge and take the first step – now! Your future awaits.

Biography for Penny & Vicky Vilagos

Business Name: Vilagos International
Address: 2975 St-Charles, Suite 218,
Kirkland QC H9H 3B5
Toll free: 1-866-426-5122
Telephone: (514) 426-5122
Fax: (514) 426-8592
Email: info@vilagosinternational.com
Web Address: www.vilagosinternational.com

Canadian Association of Professional Speakers Chapter:
Montreal. Vicky is a Professional member.

About Penny & Vicky:
Penny & Vicky Vilagos are former World Champions, Olympic medallists, authors, and bilingual motivational speakers. They work with companies who want to inspire sales team excellence, and with sales professionals who want to be champions. Keynote topics include: *With a Dream and a Plan – Yes I Can!, Champions' Competitive Edge, and Teamwork: Dreamwork.*

They are proud members of the Canadian Olympic Hall of Fame, and the Aquatic Sports Hall of Fame. Both women have Bachelor of Commerce degrees from McGill University, and 15 years of business experience. They translate *'what it takes to succeed in sports'* into *'what it takes to succeed in personal and professional endeavours.'* In 2002, Penny and Vicky were nominated as Women of Distinction in Montreal.

During her award-winning sales career, Vicky was named Sales Representative of the Year, and Sales Manager of the Year. As a professional speaker, she has served on the board for CAPS Montreal for two years. To sign up for your free ezine, visit www.vilagosinternational.com.

Other Books by Penny & Vicky:
Contributing authors to: *'Chicken Soup for the Canadian Soul®'* and
'Chicken Soup for the Sister's Soul®.'

Their upcoming book is entitled:
'Triumph Through Teamwork.'

Favourite motto: Dare to Dream!

Business Name:	Vlagos International
Address:	2975 St-Charles, Suite 216,
	Kirkland QC H9H 3B5
Toll free:	1-866-126-5122
Telephone:	(514) 426-5122
Fax:	(514) 426-8592
Email:	info@vlagosinternational.com
Web Address:	www.vlagosinternational.com

Canadian Association of Professional Speakers Chapter:
Montreal. Vicky is a Professional member.

About Penny & Vicky

Penny & Vicky Vlagos are former World Champions Olympic athletes, authors, and bilingual motivational speakers. They work with companies who want to inspire sales team excellence, and with sales professionals who want to be champions. Keynote topics include: With a Dream and a Plan to Be a Champion, Coopetition, ...

> **"Leap and the net will appear."**
> *- Julia Cameron*

They are proud members of the Canadian Olympic Hall of Fame, and the Aquatic Sports Hall of Fame. Both women have Bachelor of Commerce degrees from McGill University, and 15 years of business experience. They combine what it takes to succeed in sport, Join it takes to succeed in business and professional endeavours. In 2002, Penny and Vicky were nominated as Women of Distinction in Montreal.

During her award-winning sales career, Vicky was named Sales Representative of the Year, and Sales Manager of the Year. As a professional speaker she has served on the board for CAPS Montreal for two years. To sign up for our free ezine, visit www.vlagosinternational.com.

Other Books by Penny & Vicky
Contributing authors to: 'Chicken Soup for the Canadian Soul®' and 'Chicken Soup for the Sports Soul®'.

Their upcoming book is entitled:
'Triumph Through Teamwork'

Favourite motto: Dare to Dream!

Fitt for the Good Life

By: Maureen Hagan
MI-T-MO Enterprises Inc.,

Balance is the key to the 'Good Life'.

We all know the benefits of being fit and healthy. When asked what is important in life, 80% of us rank personal health as our first concern. In spite of this statistic, however, the health of society is worse than ever before. What we are saying, and what we are doing, are quite contradictory.

> *"The greatest irritant to most people is not the lack of money or status, but ill health. Nothing shines brightly if we do not feel well."*
>
> *- Margaret Stortz*

Many of us who are striving to achieve a healthy lifestyle are doing so for the wrong reasons. In a quest to achieve the *'super model'* body, we see in the advertising campaigns on television and in magazines, we often resort to pills and fad diets that are, in fact, counterproductive to our overall health and wellness. Not only do we fail to achieve the *'perfect body'*, but we have, in most cases, also put our health at risk. To avoid such a scenario, it is important that we understand our goals, and develop a formula for success. As you will see, the formula I promote is that of "FITT": an acronym that will be developed throughout this article.

Defining the 'Good Life'

The goal that must be first recognized and then pursued is what I have come to call the 'Good Life'. I view the Good Life as being very personal, and it is different for each of us. The Good Life consists of a healthy balance in body, mind, and spirit. To achieve this, we must combine physical fitness, healthy nutrition, and a positive attitude towards life. How this is done, and where the balance is found, is different for everyone. There is, however, one common denominator. To achieve the Good Life, we must accept personal responsibility for ourselves, and the decisions we make. Each of us must put forward the effort and motivation necessary to achieve our own optimal health and wellness.

Once we realize that we have choices and control over our own well-being, we can then understand that, with self-responsibility, and self-motivation, we can determine our own destiny and enjoy our lives to the fullest.

"It's never too late to become what you might have been."
- George Elliott

Women in the 21st century face many challenges. One of the greatest is achieving and maintaining good health throughout their lives. There is a myriad of health concerns and issues facing today's professional women, including heart disease, high blood pressure, cancer, obesity and diabetes, along with stress illness, to which women appear to be more prone than men. These concerns, together with an increased lack of healthy social and emotional relationships, are said to be even more prevalent in professional women.

In spite of these concerns, most women in today's society initially seek out fitness and exercise for the sole purpose of losing weight, and attempting to achieve the perfect body. Once women become active, however, their motivation to stay involved in fitness appears to be related not only to physical benefits, but also to emotional reasons. Women generally find they enjoy the social interaction and support they receive from others involved in fitness. They also find that when they remain active, it usually benefits both their physical and emotional well-being. Unfortunately, women are quick to give up such extra-curricular activities as going to the gym, or exercising at home, because of other priorities and commitments that arise. Having children, and increased family responsibilities, as well as the pressures of working outside the home, take priority over self-care. Too many women fail to use exercise and fitness to help address these increased pressures, and to thereby maintain healthy lifestyles. Setting aside time for physical activity should be a priority for all women.

"A sedentary lifestyle is equivalent to and has the same health risk associated with smoking a pack of cigarettes a day."
- U.S. Surgeon General Report

Effects of a Sedentary Lifestyle

If you fail to become active, your aerobic capacity will decrease at a rate of 10% per decade after the age of 25. You will find that you are breathing harder, and feeling short of breath just doing basic daily activities. Over time, such daily activities will become so strenuous that you will be unable to do them independently, or, you will be forced to avoid them completely.

Weight gain and loss of muscle strength can also be attributed to a sedentary lifestyle. We can expect to lose over one-third of our muscle during the course of our lives. This equates to losing approximately seven to ten pounds of muscle each decade, with an accelerating loss after the age of 45. Loss of muscle tissue most often leads directly to weight gain. When we lose lean muscle tissue, it negatively impacts the body's metabolism, and hence, its energy requirements for day-to-day living. The body expends fewer calories each day and, over a decade, the average person can gain up to 10 pounds of weight just as a result of the impact on the metabolism occurring due to the loss of lean muscle tissue. The average woman's body fat, as a proportion of her total body mass, will increase from 25% to 43% as she ages. This increase in body fat is, of course, associated with increases in risk of diseases related to obesity such as hypertension, coronary artery disease, osteoarthritis, diabetes, and cancer. As you lose muscle mass, you lose strength, so that by age 70, most women can expect to have 50% of the strength of a young adult.

Bone density, osteoporosis, and arthritis are also major concerns for women as they age. Bone density decreases at a rate of 1% per year after the age of 35. For women, following menopause, the loss of bone density increases, on average, to 2% per year. Brittle bones, over the long-term, can lead to fractures, disability, and loss of independence.

> **Muscle is like GOLD. It takes up a small space but is very valuable.**
>
> **Fat is like FEATHERS. It takes up space but has no value at all.**

Key Benefits of Regular Physical Activity

There are obviously some scary facts about inactivity. But, let's take some time to focus on the benefits of regular physical activity, and how it can add years to your life, and life to your years!

Women can experience incredible benefits from a regular physical fitness régime. Research studies show that women who participate in a combination of aerobic exercise and strength training for at least eight weeks can increase their overall strength by 21%, and their lean muscle tissue by 12 pounds. This is enough to burn an additional 150 calories per day. By having more muscle tissue, women will have the ability to lose weight while maintaining, or even increasing, their caloric intake. It is possible, with some planning and effort, to avoid the weight gain associated with aging altogether.

In addition, bone density will increase after only four short months of strength training, helping to offset the decrease resulting from aging as well as the incidence of chronic back pain, fibromyalgia, osteoarthritis, chronic fatigue, and the onset of diabetes. Studies support that women who exercise at least four times per week have a 37% lower risk of developing breast cancer. Exercise will reduce the risk of heart attack and stroke by 40% or more. Exercise, however, has its most profound effect in lowering the risk of colon cancer by as much as 50%. Exercise will also positively influence the challenges associated with menopause.

Stress Reduction and Regular Physical Activity

Regular physical activity also reduces the feelings and negative effects associated with stress, frustration, anger, fatigue, and depression. Stress can be defined as any state where the body is expending energy faster than it can regenerate it. In response to stress, your adrenal glands pump out a stress hormone (cortisol) that helps your body work faster. Your heart rate increases, blood sugar levels rise so that your body can divert energy fuel (glucose) to your muscles to enable you to respond to the situation. Together, these changes are known as the *fight-or-flight response.*

> *Stress can be defined as any state where the body is expending energy faster than it can regenerate it.*

Both acute and chronic stress can, however, also suppress your body's immune system. This can result in lowering your tolerance to infection and disease, including cancer. Stress is associated with the onset of allergies, arthritis, high blood pressure, and heart disease. Stress makes you tired physically, mentally, and emotionally, and can interfere with your body's sleep/wake cycle, organ function, physical performance, and feelings of well-being. Equipping your body with the tools to deal with stress is an integral step toward achieving the Good Life.

Say YES to the best, and NO to the rest.

By recognizing your priorities, and staying focused on your goals, doing work and leisure activities that you enjoy, reducing the chaos, eliminating relationships or habits that drain your energy and sabotage your self-esteem, you can improve your overall physical, mental, and emotional health. This is part of the fitness journey to the Good Life. Becoming physically active is key to burning off the stress hormones that overload the body's system. When we exercise, our bodies release endorphins, which are *feel good* chemicals that naturally counteract stress hormones. The best way to stimulate endorphins is through physical activity such as walking briskly, jogging, swimming, and cycling. In addition to these traditional forms of aerobic activity, there are a number of increasingly popular activities that help to manage or relieve stress. These activities include yoga, tai chi, meditation, deep breathing exercises and *joyful exercises* such a dancing, gardening, hiking, horseback riding and golfing. These are activities that you enjoy doing, and that give you control over your well-being. By making a decision to incorporate pleasurable activities and joyful exercise into your life, you will start to regain control, break through the vicious stress cycle, and take another step toward the Good Life.

> *"The body is the soul's house. Shouldn't we take care of our house so that it doesn't fall into ruin?"*
>
> *-Philo*

Healthy Weight Management: A Balanced Approach

As a nation, we are becoming increasingly fat. Obesity is reaching epidemic proportions in North American adults. But our bodies are amazing! While we do not know exactly why, we do know that, like our universe, our bodies strive for balance. Any fitness, nutrition, or lifestyle program that limits a key element, component, or skill will wreak havoc with our bodies. Any diet that limits a key nutrient will cause the same chaos within our bodies.

Vitamins, minerals, water, carbohydrates, protein, and fat are essential nutrients required in balance to maintain equilibrium in our bodies. This equilibrium is known as *homeostasis*. If you deprive your body of any of the essential nutrients, it will rebel! The key to improving health, and increasing fat loss, is to combine an increase in physical activity with a program of strength training and at the same time, adjust your diet to decrease your caloric intake.

Calories are important players in the energy balance formula. They are the fuel that allows your body to operate. However, consuming 3,500 calories more than what you actually require will produce an extra one pound of fat. Similarly, reducing your intake of calories by 3,500 will result in weight loss. This means 500 calories less each day for a week results in one pound of fat loss. This, of course, seems insignificant when compared to the 10 pounds or more that can be lost if the claims of the fad diets are to be believed. Such rapid weight loss promised by, and in some cases even delivered by, the fad diets, does, however, have one problem. The weight comes back!

Balance is the Key

The key to successful weight loss is balance. By restricting caloric intake by more than 500 calories a day, you cause a reduction in your metabolic rate. Your *metabolic rate* is the rate at which your body burns calories as fuel during a day. If the objective is fat loss, then the goal must be to increase your metabolic rate, and burn more calories each day. Decreasing calories by too much, too fast, causes your body to conserve energy by, in fact, burning fewer calories. This is known as the *starvation syndrome*. The most effective way to increase your metabolic rate is to increase your muscle tissue mass. Muscle works like your car engine – the larger the engine, the more fuel it burns. The average female burns approximately 1,200 to 1,500 calories a day. Add an extra pound of muscle, and there is an increase of 70 to 100 additional calories burned just to maintain that increased muscle. Strength training is the vehicle to muscle gain, and lean muscle is the path to fat loss. In the long term, it is much more effective to gain muscle and, thus, increase your metabolism, than just to try to dieting alone.

Canada's Food Guide recommends that 40% - 50% of your daily calories should come from carbohydrates (fruits, vegetables, and whole grains); 20% - 30% should come from protein (lean meat, fish, eggs, dairy, soy products, beans, legumes, nuts and seeds), and 20% - 30% should come from fat (olive, flaxseed, canola oils, as well as fat that comes from carbohydrate and protein sources). You can help your metabolism to work effectively by eating smaller, more frequent balanced meals following the Food Guide. This concept is generally known as 'grazing'. Keep your engine tuned up underneath the body surface, and you are on your way to the Good Life.

Putting It All Together

To try to put all of the principles of the Good Life together, you need to think of **FITT** as a formula to follow.

F (Frequency): Frequency refers to the number of times per week you should participate in a physical activity. Begin with three times per week, plus two walks and, within six weeks, progress to five times per week. Incorporate physical activity into each day where possible such as using the stairs rather than the elevator.

I (Intensity): Intensity refers to the level of exertion experienced. You should engage in the activity to a level that you perceive to be somewhat strenuous (breathing harder than normal, heart rate elevated, and a light sweat occurs).

T (Time): This is the length of time you are engaged in the exercise or physical activity. Begin with 15 - 20 minutes of sustained, continuous activity at the desired intensity. It may require you to warm-up for five minutes, and recover for another five minutes for a total of 30 minutes. Progress in one of two ways:

- repeat the activity twice per day (before and after work), or
- engage in a single session for a minimum of 30 minutes, building to 60 minutes within a six-week training period.

T (Type): Choose a type of exercise or physical activity that you love, or think you will enjoy. Include both aerobic and strength training exercises, and remember to stretch after each session or throughout the day. Stretching will relieve muscle soreness and fatigue, as well as maintain joint mobility and flexibility. Be aware that if you have any special needs, limitations, or health concerns, you must first consult with your health professional before beginning an exercise program. This person should be able to design a program addressing your special needs, or to refer you to someone who can.

Small changes bring about large differences.

Build physical activity into your day and your travel plans. Imagine how much better you will feel when you stand, walk, and sit taller; with your shoulders back, chest proud, abdominals pulled in, and buttocks toned and tight. Go for a walk, or light jog, or engage in light physical activity immediately following a long drive or flight. This will help reduce the symptoms associated with jet lag, and traveler's lethargy. Break up your day with fitness breaks or physical activity before, during, and after work. Three sessions of 10 minutes each has proven to be as effective as doing a one 30-minute session. You will feel stronger, have more energy, and be more efficient. You will be quicker in your step, more agile in your daily activities, and you will be able to do daily work with much less exertion. You will feel less anxious, and have less stress. You will experience a greater sense of self-confidence, have more energy, and a positive attitude. Successfully achieving the Good Life begins with you!

> **Your attitude towards life determines your altitude in life.**

Success is a journey, not a destination.

Success is not just a set of achievements, and it is not found in the world around you, but rather, it comes from within. To view success in your life as a journey represents an amazing shift in thinking for some people. You have likely witnessed this first hand in your professional career. Your desire to achieve personal and professional excellence requires commitment, perseverance, peak attitude, integrity, and hard work. The same formula is required in order for you to succeed in your personal life, and to ensure you achieve the Good Life.

You may be thinking that all this sounds great, and perhaps you would like to embark on a fitness program. At the same time, however, you may also be saying to yourself, 'I simply don't have time'. This is the number one excuse for not starting, or for quitting, an exercise program. There is, however, an interesting fact about time, and those who strive for the Good Life:

> *At a minimum, you are 20% more productive if you exercise regularly. This means you create 33 more hours per week by being fit. By investing as little as one, two to three hours of exercise per week, you can gain the equivalent of 33 hours a week in terms of productivity. Where do those 33 hours come from? You get them because your decisions are 20% faster, you have 20% less anxiety, and your sleep is 20% better. Absenteeism from work will drop, and your attitude towards life will increase your commitment to doing in leaps and bounds that which you use to do at a snail's pace.*

Add years to your life and life to your years.

It is not surprising that when you make changes in your life, whether it is making fitness a part of your lifestyle, or making changes in your business, you may not see the results or reap the rewards immediately. Researchers have found ONE significant characteristic common to all those who succeed in making exercise a part of their lives. Those people move towards their goal one step at a time. Those people are committed to making improvements, regardless of busy work or travel schedules, lack of energy, lack of time, feeling lazy, or hating exercise, they make no excuses! They just do it!

The Good Life is a journey mapped by the quality of the goals, choices, and decisions that you make for yourself, and what you contribute to your journey. Perseverance is one of your contributions to the path towards those goals. By participating in regular physical activity, and conducting yourself in a healthy manner, most age-related changes can be prevented, or at least their impact delayed and lessened.

There is a checklist to which successful participants in exercising generally subscribe. Not all of these points apply to everyone, but in almost every case, at least one of these points plays a role in the success of the participant.

- Commit to making new habits! It takes at least 21 days to change a habit, or to adopt a new one, and at least six weeks to see the results of your efforts. Do not let what you cannot do stand in the way of the things you can do!
- Make it a goal, write it down with a deadline, and accompany it with the benefits that you will have once the goal is achieved. Share it with someone supportive in your life, and have *them* hold you accountable for achieving that goal by the set deadline.
- Eat a healthy and significant breakfast, eat a moderate lunch, and very light dinner. In this fashion, you will intake most of your calories during the day when you are active, and burning them off, rather than at night, when you are inactive and storing them. In other words, eat like a queen at breakfast, a princess at lunch and Cinderella at dinner. Drink more water. You are what you eat (and drink).
- Be active each day. Park your car further away from your destination, and walk. Take the stairs instead of the elevator. Walk for leisure, go for hikes, garden, take dance lessons, or join a club (golf, fitness, bowling, ski).

- Choose activities that you enjoy, and that you can do with family or friends. Participate for as little as 15 minutes in light physical activity directly following your evening meal to curb cravings, burn more calories, relax you and improve the quality of your sleep. Light household chores, gardening, walking around the block will do just fine.
- Keep a daily exercise/physical activity and nutrition log. By recording your activities and your food intake, you will be more successful. Most people overestimate their activity levels by 50%, and underestimate their caloric intake by 30%. Be diligent in your recording, and do not lie to yourself.
- Sleep long enough and at consistent times each night to enjoy the benefits (i.e. minimum of eight hours starting at 10:00 p.m.).
- Manage your stress by identifying it. Reframe it by taking control at the onset of stress through taking a deep breath, and calming yourself down. Neutralize the effects of stress by doing something for fun every day.
- Change or improve your mind using the techniques of visualization, and imagination. Similar to an athlete who visualizes and imagines receiving the gold medal on the podium, see yourself doing the activity, and feeling energized. Think about how it felt the last time you engaged in that activity and relive in your mind those feelings of enjoyment, pride, and success. In your mind's eye, experience doing the activity to the best of your ability. Believe it or not, you will not only look forward to the actual experience, you will also be more successful, because your mind is helping direct your actions.
- Success breeds success! Monitor and reward yourself for successes, however small or insignificant they seem along the way. Find yourself a mentor, coach, or friend who inspires you. Make small changes one step at a time, and stay the course. Never give up. Think of every day as a new day, and a new opportunity and you will be amazed at your results. Your beliefs will direct your mind, and your actions will follow!

> *"If you think you can do something or if you think you can't do something, you're right in both cases."*
> *— Henry Ford*

Think of your actions as things that you want to do, versus things that you would rather avoid. Think about the things that you want and that are good for you, and your mind will, in turn, create good cravings. Remember, too, that taking action is about taking responsibility for your life. The extent to which you are willing to act is equal to how much you are exercising your *'pro-activity'* muscles. Developing these muscles is comparable to developing any other muscles. It takes time to see the results. Do not give up, because it will certainly be worth the time and effort.

> **Your destination is determined by the power from within.**

The Good Life is attainable for those who understand it, and take the positive steps to achieve it.

Yours in fitness and good health.

Recommended Readings

Kwasnicki, Sheri	*Go For Fit – The Winning Way To Fat Loss,* by Raincoast Publishing
McMillan, Sherri	*Fit Over Forty – The Winning Way To Lifetime Fitness,* by Raincoast Publishing
Patchell-Evans, David	*Living The Good Life – Your Guide To Health and Success,* by Stoddart Publishing

Biography for Maureen Hagan

Business Name: MI-T-MO Enterprises Inc.
Address: 248 Pall Mall Street, Suite 402
London, Ontario N6A 5P6
Telephone: (519) 439-4267
Fax: (519) 439-0788
E-mail: mo@goodlifefitness.com
Web address: www.mohagan.com

Canadian Association of Professional Speakers Chapter:
Southwestern Ontario. Professional member

About Maureen:

Maureen Hagan, BScPT, BA P.E., ACE and Can Fit Pro Certified, is Vice President - Operations, Group EX for the Good Life Fitness Clubs, and Director of Education for CAN FIT PRO - Canadian Fitness Professionals. Maureen is an international educator and fitness professional trainer.

She travels worldwide training fitness instructors. Maureen's physiotherapy training and 20 years of teaching experience have gained her expertise in all areas of the fitness and health profession. Maureen is a national speaker with CAPS and a Canadian sponsored '3 Stripe Athlete' with adidas. She is also the recipient of the 1996 Educator of the Year - Bodylife Germany; 1997 Canadian Presenters Choice Award winner; and 1998 IDEA International Program Director of the Year.

The Power Of You

By: Terri Knox
Service Enhanced Training

Learn to harness the powerful forces in your life.

Being the youngest of 11 children is called survival. My parents came to Canada in 1952 with 10 children (I was born after they arrived), two suitcases, and thirty-five dollars. When they went to the Canadian immigration office, the only language they knew was Dutch.

It's amazing how a family could pick up and move across the world with so little – leaving their families, their country, and their language. Everything they knew was forever gone. Thankfully, the church took in this huge family and put them on a farm in rural Saskatchewan. The entire family worked the farm in repayment for lodging and food. We have colonies to this day that do this, and yet, in 1952, it was so surreal.

When we take shortcuts in life to get to the good stuff, we have not travelled our full journey.

My Mom always kept one suitcase packed, and would never let anyone open or empty it. That way, she thought, she could be ready to go home in an instant. I remember her telling me how she would stand in the middle of a farmyard, yelling up at the sky to her sisters and brothers. She was telling them how much she longed for them and her home.

Having enough food on a daily basis was a challenge we accomplished with gardening and hard work. We certainly did not have time nor money for a pet, so how we happened to obtain a canary was beyond me. One day, someone let the canary out, and it flew into my Mom's pot of chicken soup…no, not for the soul! My Mom ever so gently plucked it out and, as we buried this little critter, she continued with the same pot of soup. Imagine!

My Mom was able to serve the most interesting dinners, even though life was very difficult. She prided herself in always having dessert for us, but her problem was that we did not have enough plates. We had to flip our dinner plate over so our dessert could be placed on the backside of it. My Mom figured this was okay, because, then, we would have to eat our entire dinner before we could receive dessert. Little did she know that I mastered flipping this thing over quite efficiently with food still on it. Little did I know she was on to me... I still remember the consequences.

I now realize that, when we take short cuts in life to get to the good stuff, we have not travelled our full journey. Having learned to 'cut the short cuts' and take the long road, I find I appreciate things more now. I also know I continue to heed this lesson constantly in order to honor my journey. Every once in a while – *after* I've finished my entire dinner – I will flip over my plate for dessert even though a stack of clean dishes is in my cupboard!

I've learned that in order to survive life, we do whatever needs to be done to make it happen. Challenging as it may sometimes be, taking the long-road rather than the shortcut in life puts us on the path of constant learning and new life experiences. It is what our life journey is all about. Without challenges to teach us life lessons, we would just exist in our physical shells.

The Power of... Your Faith

Our life was hard, but we were all fed and clothed. Our parents also taught us that Christianity was the core of our family. As a child, I went to church every morning and Benediction every Saturday. Back then, everything was in Latin, and I didn't really understand the reality of faith and prayer. As a family, we said the rosary every night, and kneeling on the register meant the Lord would hear our prayers more effectively.

As an adult, I was able to learn so much more about faith, and church, and prayer. My own faith is something I now honour and cherish. While it is important to respect the faith of all other individuals, to understand and honour one's own meaning of life is truly rewarding. My own understanding of it all is much deeper, and my faith now is the very base of my existence. Without it, I wouldn't be able to live the life I live, and do what I love to do each day. Growing up, I also didn't understand how to 'free flow' in prayer – to me, every prayer was rhetorical. It took me many years to develop a prayerful relationship, which has enhanced my life.

> **We've all heard that laughter is the best medicine, but I personally find that prayer is the best medicine to administer in good and bad times.**

It is amazing how, when most individuals are in deep trouble, their spirituality suddenly becomes much stronger. Thank heaven that God has a great sense of humour, and keeps no scorecard! How interesting it is, too, when so often in life, we tend to measure and keep score of all our experiences – especially the unpleasant ones.

The Power of… Forgiveness

We've all regretted, at one time or another, something we shouldn't have done or said, or perhaps something we *did* do or say. At least I hope we all have – I would love to meet the perfect individual who has never done anything to be remorseful about! Then again, maybe not!

> To forgive – to stop being resentful of, or angry at something or someone, *including ourselves* – is such an intricate and necessary part of one's life.

Having the ability to do this does not mean that we go through life looking for people to 'take shots' at us. We need to put in safety devices and protect ourselves, but the need to forgive is essential. When we forgive, we release ourselves from our emotional prisons so we can move forward. Many people go through life angry for years at someone or something. If only these people could recognize the loss they are experiencing! Forgiving and learning to let go of anger can be a tremendous healing power for our souls.

The Power of… Your Journey

So, why am I sharing this background with all who come across this dynamic book? We need to recognize the journey in life will always be ours.

My parents' journey led them to an incredible amount of hard work and pain, especially for my Mom. The power within this woman was amazing. When she died at the early age of 64, she was said to die of a worn out heart. Her heart didn't even have the strength to have a heart attack!

Giving birth to 11 children, suffering two miscarriages, and having, on average, at least eight boarders for well over 10 years was an abnormal load for anyone to carry. This incredible woman also, at age 12, had rheumatic fever, which left her with only two out of four heart valves working properly. Now, had the husband of most women come home to say the entire family was moving clear across the world, I am quite sure most of us would have told him to write when he got there!

One of the most paralyzing thoughts that we carry is that, even though we are a product of our environment, we also have the ability to make it better. Being chained to the past is a crippling disease, and claims our ability to be the best at who we are. I remember my Mom telling me that "everyone's happiness depended on me." How frightening can *that* be for any individual – especially for my Mom, who continued this false belief all her life.

We tend to be so busy 'emotionally tap-dancing' in life, trying to be everything to everyone: our partners, children, friends, colleagues, and community. No wonder that we neglect 'speed bumps' and forget that our life is the most miraculous lesson we will ever receive.

The Power of… Relief

No, I'm not talking about *Rolaids*™! I'm talking about the internal and external relief experienced when you release pent-up feelings. These feelings can include those of anger, hurt, confusion, frustration, or the 'stop the world I want to get off' feeling we get once in a while.

Recognizing these emotional barriers, and releasing and letting go of them, can bring powerful and tremendous relief to our physical and mental beings. Sometimes, what's put the barrier in place is something you'd never imagined. And, sometimes, recognizing and releasing them can happen when you least expect it:

> *I was in a community, presenting to a group where one would usually see me with a lot of power and strength. As the result of certain personal decisions I had previously made, I was overwhelmed with feelings that were affecting me.*
>
> *To help with these feeling, after the presentation, I chose to go for a drive. My sense of direction is not very good, and in my attempt to find inner peace, I got more lost. I saw an interesting church and went in seeking some direction – physically and emotionally. The janitor saw my plight, and suggested that I speak to the minister, not realizing that my real concern was finding my way back to the hotel.*
>
> *I was surprised to see this minister, well into his seventies, looking so wise and patient. As we talked, he inquired*

as to what I did for a living. He also noted that there appeared to be some similarities in our desire to share with others. He then inquired, "Do you at times become overwhelmed?" which was quite obvious. He then asked me one of the most profound questions that I have ever been asked, "Who takes care of the caregiver?" I was speechless. At that moment I realized that my well was dry. I was not making good choices in life because I had not honoured whom I was.

Many times, caregivers give and try to be everything to everyone. We try to make a difference in people's lives by being the caregiver of all who encounter us. How simple, yet so complex! Celebrate you and honour your gift of life.

**Life is the greatest gift given, and how we
live our life is the greatest gift returned.**

The Power of... Your Inner Self

I have a picture of myself at age four, 'mooning' for all to see. How else was I to get anyone's attention? We do many things in life to get attention. While this may be a survival method for some, it also can cause a long range of emotional problems.

Our success in life begins with taking an inventory of what is going on inside. If we do not like whom we are, how is it possible to be of significance to others? How are we able to be healthy partners, parents, friends, and community members, when we cannot be good to the best friend that we will ever have...ourselves?

My Mom believed and taught me that it was selfish to be self-focused. I now realize that it is more selfish *not* to be. When we travel to the place of being *self-centered*, rather than *self-focused*, then we are heading for problems. Self-centered is best described as what is best for you in the short run: self-focused is what is most important in the long-term. Attempting to achieve harmony in light of our circumstances with those around us is essential.

My father used to say, *"little kids, little problems...big kids, big problems"*. I used to think it was unfortunate that he had no idea what he was talking about. How ironic it is though, as we only recognize that our parents seem to get smarter (even in death) as we grow older. As I travel my journey in life, I'm amazed at how we 'get it together' as we grow older. What a promising thought that is!

> When you take care of that inner self
> inside of you, your outer self can't help but
> reflect it. You have the constant reminder
> of how the best friend you will ever have in
> your life, one that will stand by you
> forever, is you.

The Power of… Your Thought

So how *do* we capture our internal strength and develop it on an ongoing basis? It starts with a lifelong commitment. We certainly have challenges along the way. But, I also believe this allows us to pay attention. Many years ago, Henry Ford made a statement that still remains true:

If you think that you can or you can't, you're right!

So often, our power of thought controls the successes we have or the ones we miss.

Throughout high school, I was led to believe that school was a huge social event. My Mom kept encouraging me to quit school, and get a job to earn money. Education wasn't a factor in my parents' minds, because it wasn't part of their environment. But, how could I quit school when I was having so much fun? Most of my teachers tolerated me, as I made them laugh, but my lack of commitment was very frustrating for them. My closest friends couldn't understand why I was not in the regular classes – I always seemed to end up in the 'zoo rooms', as they were called. As a result, I was labeled a slow learner, and, because someone made that assessment, I decided they must be right.

Wrong! I wasted so many opportunities during those precious years. I know that we cannot un-ring a bell, but I still feel a sense of loss at what my true abilities were. Many things, and ways we think, can determine our outcome, until the very end of our lives. At the tender age of 18, I was hired by Air Canada as a flight attendant. They immediately sent me for six weeks of grueling training courses. I had to achieve a passing mark of 80%, or I was out! I wanted this career so badly, that I forgot what most adults had me believe during my high school years. Buckling down to my studies, I walked away with a 96% average, and never looked back as to my level of intelligence.

How often do we want to tackle a career, or relationship, believing that we may not be well enough equipped? Even though someone may tell me I am not qualified to be a surgeon, I know I can tackle most anything if I want it bad enough. I had never visualized myself as a public speaker, but, certainly, now recognize that it was always there. Every job I ever had in my life I made it my favourite – from carrying trays at a banquet hall to public speaking. I've been so fortunate! So, what *are* the lessons that we are here to learn? How *do* we cope and handle the pain and happiness that flow through our journey in life?

The Power of…The Lessons

Every day, people all over the world are told they have a terminal disease, or that their chemotherapy isn't working. Why is it then, as I write this chapter, I am so distraught because an airline lost my baggage for three days?

Having been in the airline industry for many years, and dealing with individuals who lose their possessions, I find it ironic that, as I write, it is I who am experiencing this situation. The fact that two thousand dollars worth of clothing disappeared put my life into a tailspin. I am not enjoying a special mini-vacation with my husband, because I am fretting the entire time, knowing I cannot replace the expensive outfits I use in my profession as a public speaker. And yet, I know that so often, others have lost luggage, where it is not the dollar amount but the memorable things that had meant so much.

How sad it is for me to realize that this non life-threatening situation has invaded my spirit! I did not respond well to this simple life lesson. As I write, I now realize that *only I* am in control as to how I respond to this, or any situation. I am taking back my control, which I had so freely and easily given up. I now recognize in my heart that, if my suitcase is meant to return to me, it certainly will.

Even though one feels anger, anguish, and dismay in this situation, the reality is that the importance of what is lost is based on how we feel about them. If a person can stay focused and accept the loss, it is easier to maintain a positive spirit. An interesting question to ponder is: *'Are the lost articles or clothing you, or are you the clothing?'*

Maintaining my spirit, I will now use this as another speed bump in life. To honor and recognize my response to this is nothing short of a miracle. As we journey through life, often we do not recognize the lessons put forward to us every day. Our response to these situations is what determines our successes or failures. When we experience the loss of a relationship, job, or even a suitcase with our possessions, often we immediately 'knee-jerk' to our unpleasant situation. We wouldn't deliberately choose many of these experiences, but I believe we need to respond to everything, and every situation, with our head and heart, rather than solely our emotions. So, what is the best healer? Having faith in *self* is certainly a start.

> **One of the best healers in life is called time, and yet we very seldom take time to recognize this.**

There are situations where we can't imagine things being worse, but they can be. Though the reality of our lives can challenge us, it is key to remember that only '*we*' are in control of our response to any situation – and thus can make the situation better or worse ourselves.

The Power of... Your Attitude

I remember one day asking a very good, single friend, *"Aren't you lonely?"* Her response was very educational for me, and remains embedded in my mind. She said, *"I'd rather be lonely with myself, than lonely with someone else."* What an eye-opener – talk about attitude!

Recognizing your strongest qualities calls for a 'heads-up' attitude. And finding your own personal strength is one of the greatest accomplishments you can achieve. Fine tuning this strength is essential. Positive attitudes trigger enthusiasm and enhance creativity. You can create positive attitudes by critically eyeing your strengths and weaknesses. You can learn to examine your beliefs and influences. Why is it that some individuals manage to become successful, while others remain shackled by paralyzing doubt? So many people – especially women – lose incredible opportunities by not recognizing and utilizing their own strengths.

It took me many years to figure out why I always had a need to surround myself with people. So much so that, there are times when, 'anyone would do'. You need not live in an environment – mentally or physiologically – that does not generate growth and fulfillment. Often, we surround ourselves with situations or individuals that de-motivate us, or stop us from achieving what we want to accomplish. (Sometimes the need to have certain people in our lives tends to be very toxic.) Clearly looking at how and whom you surround yourself with is critical. *How* you respond to what you find out can have an incredible impact on your attitude toward your inner self, and those you choose to be with.

The Power of… Yourself

I realize that, more than anything, I need to hear my own message. Renowned author Steven Covey says, *"We tend to teach what we most need to learn."* What an incredible insight! Now, I make a date, at least once a week, with my best friend to do something together. My best friend happens to be *me*. I can truly say that having lunch and going for walks – *with me* – is wonderful therapy. Getting to know *me* has been phenomenal.

Through enjoying a healthy relationship with ourselves, we are much more equipped to achieve our goals. We're also better to those who surround our lives – both personally, and professionally. And, taking responsibility for our own behaviour when things are not going smoothly is another critical life lesson. Until we can accept responsibility for – and the consequences of – our actions and choices, we cannot really be sure our life is going in the right direction. We have to recognize that *we* are the architects of our lives. How we live life is determined by the many choices we face every day. If we are not truly happy, we need to take a good look at why. We also need to figure out what we can do to change this.

In many cases, such as a working environment, we are placed in people's lives that we might personally never choose to be with. So, how do we cope in a toxic work environment? Know that we are never in control of how someone treats or speaks to us, but we are in control of our own response. This is true growth. Know, too, that this is a lifelong challenge, and there are always going to be many individuals or situations that constantly test our responses.

The most challenging people in my life have given me the most growth. I certainly know that one would not go out looking for individuals like this, but the reality is that they will find *us*. Here are two suggestions for this type of situation:

1. We can treat this as a life lesson and ask ourselves, what *are they here to teach us?*

2. We can step back and not do the 'knee–jerk' reaction. Responding by stepping back usually shocks this type of individual. They are looking for confrontation and we *don't have* to accommodate them.

One of my short-term goals – *every day* – is to make the most miserable person I encounter, smile. It is sometimes a challenge, but what a self-motivator when it's accomplished! There are so many suggestions for personal power in this book – hopefully not overwhelming. I personally do not want to complete all of life's lessons – they are what makes my journey so wonderful. My favourite story, which I share at many presentations, is this:

> *A small African-American child was sitting on a set of steps across from Central Park in New York. Now, people make their living in some very unusual ways at Central Park. On this particular day, a man was selling helium balloons, but business was not very good. The man would periodically release a balloon and people watched it rise into the air, then came to his vending station to buy one.*
>
> *As the small child watched, the man released a yellow balloon, then a white one, a green one and a blue one. The little boy jumped off the steps and walked into the park and up to the man at the vending station. He tugged at the man's shirt and said, "Excuse me, mister?" The man looked down at the little boy and replied, "Yes, son?"*
>
> *The little boy asked, "Sir, you have a black balloon tied to your machine there. If you were to let it go, would it go up also?" The man was very intrigued and he bent down and looked into the small child's eyes. Then he responded, "Son, it's not the colour of the balloon that makes it go up, it's what's inside!"*
>
> *- Original Source Unknown*

It does not matter your race, age, hair or eye colour, how big or small you are. It's what's inside of you that counts. Every one of you reading this book has the power to recognize how truly special *you* are, and how much *you need you.*

You can't do it without you!

Biography for Terri Knox

Business Name:	Service Enhanced Training
Address:	34 Hennessey Drive,
	Winnipeg, Manitoba
	R3P 1P8
Telephone:	(204) 488-1171
Toll Free:	1-877-488-1171
Fax:	(204) 488-2508
Email:	terri@terriknox.com
Web Address:	www.terriknox.com

Canadian Association of Professional Speakers Chapter:
Winnipeg, Professional Member

About Terri:

Terri Knox has accumulated a wealth of experience while dealing with the public in her 22 years in the airline industry. Terri was the coordinator of Education and Training for the Tourism Industry. Nominated Female Entrepreneur of the Year, Terri's successful company – Service Enhanced Training – has been bringing inspirational keynotes and seminars to a wide variety of clients of every sector across North America.

Terri provides you with tips to increase your self-image, develop goal-setting techniques and enables you to achieve personal success. Her messages will lead to enhanced relationships professionally and personally. Her major areas of expertise are: personal development, self-image, and customer relations.

Terri is a strong believer in positive reinforcement to enhance our skills and one who believes that in today's competitive economy, the key to increasing your bottom line will be super-exceeding customer service expectations.

Audio Programs by Terri:

'Tools for Success' (tape & CD)

"Trust in yourself. Your perceptions are often far more accurate than you are willing to believe."

- *Claudia Black*

How to Stay Cool When Your Pants are On Fire

By: Arlene Jorgenson
HEALTHSERVE Saskatchewan Limited

Energy Savers for busy women

In the early 1990's, when I was an occupational health nurse for the federal government in Manitoba, the most frequently requested workshop I had was 'Stress Management'. At the time 'stress' and 'burn-out' were new-fashioned words. I faithfully – and, I would like to think, skillfully – put on interactive, fun-filled workshops for workers. I believed my courses would change their lives, and help them cope better with the ever-mounting stresses of downsizing, restructuring, layoffs, and cutbacks.

Enthusiastically, I taught techniques such as deep breathing and visualization that current thinking promised would aid weary and overwrought souls to find peace and balance amidst the turmoil of their work lives. *("In through your nose...out through your mouth...in through your nose...")*. At the same time, a book by Dr. Peter Hanson, *'The Joy of Stress'*, was flying off the shelves with practical theories on building up our resistance to stress with enough sleep, good food, and respecting that we need time to recover, in body and soul, from stressful events. All of these ideas were great, but somehow, I felt I was missing something. Successful stress management had to be more than a series of techniques.

Getting Older and Better

Life has a way of taking the shiny edge off of our náiveté. I have emerged into a new millennium older and much more sober about the realities of our struggle with the inevitable ebb and flow of living. With this comes the realization that my grip on life needs to be lighter, not tighter. There is no point in getting older and worse, so my quest has been to get older and better! I imagine that this is your quest too!

Teaching people how to 'keep their pants from catching fire' in the first place might seem to make more sense. And maybe it would be a hot seller (pardon the bad pun)! It is sound occupational health practise to prevent the accident in the first place! My sense is that this would be as successful as signing me up for the latest fad diet – nice idea on paper but on close inspection anyone can see that I'm not likely to be victorious!

As human beings, we have a lot of good intentions. But, in our hurry-scurry world, when our heads are down and our noses to the grindstone, what we really need is to be reminded of the basics. We need to create the mind-set that will bring us back to our true values. To help with this, here is a summary of my ABC's for keeping cool when your pants are on fire. While reading this chapter, see if it reminds you of your true values.

'A' is for Attitude

"Come and play Barbies, Auntie Arlene", invited my five year old niece, Hanna, from the living room, where she and her older brother were playing. I made an excuse about needing to finish cleaning up in the kitchen first. "Come on, just sit down and play Barbies with us, Auntie," she pleaded again and again. Finally, I relented and joined them on the floor with the pile of Barbie clothes and dolls. I wasn't excited about it, because I really didn't know how to play Barbies. I was the oldest child from a hard working farm family. I don't remember playing Barbies; I just remember working!

So, I looked at the pile of Barbie dolls and clothes, and thought what my first move should be. One option would be to observe the other participants and model their behaviour. A few questions of inquiry might help: is there an objective? is there a destination? is there dialogue? "Oh, Auntie Arlene, you just play Barbies!" Hanna instructed.

Apparently, the only purpose of playing Barbies is to put their clothes on and take them off. When you have mixed and matched a good outfit, and found shoes to go with it, you hold your Barbie up and 'show' everyone how nice it looks. Then, you rip it off and start hunting for another ensemble. You also have to help Ken, because Ken has trouble finding enough outfits! I was feeling quite pleased with myself, mixing, matching, showing, helping Ken, when all of a sudden, my 5-going-on-25-year-old niece said, "Oh, Auntie Arlene, that doesn't match!" How soon they learn there is a way to make it more complicated!

The objective was to have fun! Do you remember when your parents said, *"We will support you, whatever path you choose in life; as long as you're having fun and enjoying what you're doing."* We've forgotten that! Our lives have become complicated, over-scheduled and way too serious! Don't get me wrong – I think we should take our work seriously, but it is dangerous to take ourselves too seriously. It kills joy, it kills spontaneity, and it kills fun. Has anyone said to you lately, "You're no fun anymore?" Ouch! It's time to adjust our attitudes, and start to lighten up, loosen up, and be more 'goofy'. We need to become more acquainted with fun, play, and recreation.

Families that play together, stay together!

Exercise: What are the things that make you smile, laugh, and bring you joy? Make a list, and you can use the space below to write it down.

Now, make a point of doing those things more often. Plan them into your schedule, and guard them as closely as you guard your obligations to those significant people in your life. You would never think of letting-down your loved ones, so don't short-change yourself! This responsibility is to your own wellness!

'B' Fix Your Brakes, Not Your Accelerator

**If you know what your destination is,
Then it's easy to say NO to the things that
won't get you there.**

After working for five years as a community health nurse in northern Saskatchewan, and in the North West Territories, I found myself packing for Winnipeg, Manitoba the day after Christmas in 1985. My (then) pilot husband had received an attractive job offer to fly with the corporate fleet of a large company. Moving 'south' was the goal of most government people up north, so I should have been happy. My qualifications as a nurse allowed me to transfer with the government, and start work immediately in an occupational health nurse position.

Five years later, I was back in Saskatoon, with another transfer and a promotion, and supervising staff with the determination to get my life back on track after leaving my abusive husband. In my frenzy to prove myself, I often worked late, or took work home. I regularly over-scheduled myself, resulting in the stress of being late or missing appointments. I said '*yes*' to every request, because I was desperate for everyone to like me. I took my job and myself very, very seriously. My degrees and certificates were lined up on the wall behind my desk, hoping to prove that I was a good nurse, and a good person.

As a consequence, I ended up being exactly like many of the workers who came to see me through the Employee Assistance Program. I was suffering the physical and emotional symptoms of ill health that we often lump together in the non-specific term of burn-out.

These symptoms had come on so gradually, and become so routine, that I accepted them as 'normal': daily headaches, weight gain, food binges, waking up exhausted, no matter how much I slept. I covered the dark circles under my eyes believing it was just 'my fair colouring'. I put up with regular skin breakouts and rashes, thinking it was 'just hormones'. I forfeited family gatherings and babysitting my new nephews because I was 'so busy'. As a 'smart nurse', I was sure all I needed was a weekend of sleep, and everything would be fine! My counsellor finally got me to agree that I was not well, and that it was okay to take some time off. I didn't know then that it would be three months before I would feel completely well!

I learned that there is no shame in getting to the end of your rope, and feeling like you are completely losing it. But, for goodness sake, tie a knot in the end of that rope so that whenever you get close to it again, you will feel it, and not let yourself go any further. I still work hard at my career, but at the top of my goal sheet for each year is 'Prevent Burn-out – Continuous Renewal'. And, I've never let that kind of burnout sabotage me again.

As women in this day and age, we can aspire to have anything we want. But NOT ALL AT THE SAME TIME! Fix your brakes, not your accelerator.

Here are some great ideas – many that women have shared in my seminars – to help learn how to fix your brakes.

Top 10 Ways to Fix Your Brakes

1. *Turn it off!* We turn off our answering machine before we go on vacation. Who needs to come home to two weeks of messages that are too old, or too late, and feel guilty?

2. *Leave it!* Leave work at work: keep it from spilling over into your 'home-time'.

3. *Unplug it!* We unplug our phone during supper hour. Family time is too valuable to allow interruptions.

4. *Turn it down!* I don't listen to the radio in my vehicle. I value the quiet time to think instead.

5. *Unclutter!* Use the 'one-year' rule: anything that hasn't been used or worn in the past year needs to be tossed, sold, recycled, or given away.

6. *Use technology carefully!* I have a cell phone, but only my office and my husband have the number. I don't want to be available all the time.

7. *Match your goals with your desired workload!* We have always dreamed of a cabin at the lake but realized we could rent many, many times before it would be worth the cost and headache of buying one.

8. *Banish perfectionist ideals!* I may tidy up for company, but five minutes after they arrive, no one notices! They came for the hospitality, not to inspect your house cleaning.

9. *Just say 'No'!* They don't want to hear all your excuses, so just say, 'Thank you but, no, I/we aren't going to participate this year.' Then drop it!

10. *Think twice – leap once!* It can take years to get off those committees that you've outgrown. It takes five minutes to sign up for the one thing you are ready, willing and waiting for!

'C' Commit to Being an Encourager

> It's a no-brainer to be a complainer.
> But, it takes some thought to
> Give praise and thanks where you ought to.

When I married my 'new' wonderful husband, Stu, it was a package deal. He brought with him adult children, their spouses, and a lovely assortment of grandchildren. I don't have children, so this leap into 'grandma-hood' was quite startling!

One day, my grandson, Shaun, called me on the phone. He was about two and a half at the time. I didn't know it was him at first, because he couldn't really talk yet. I could just hear this little breathing, and I could hear his mom in the background, encouraging him, "Tell Grandma what you did." I soon caught onto what was really happening, and put on my grandma voice. With me encouraging him from this end, and his mom encouraging him from the other end, finally, he told me what he had called to tell me he had done. 'POOP!' Well! Because I am his grandma, I knew exactly what that meant: Shaun did a poop in the potty! So I cheered and clapped and praised him, and told him what a big boy he was. Then I called for Grandpa, so he could hear this important news first hand!

With little kids, we understand the connection between encouragement and building up self-esteem. This, in turn, builds up self-confidence, which in turn, will give them a solid foundation for successful lives. We give them stickers and stars; we put their artwork on the fridge. We are there at every little piano recital and hockey game, cheering and videotaping. Around grade five or six, we stop doing the stickers and the stars. Researchers say that it's around then that kids start having trouble with self-esteem, especially girls, and we know that this is not right.

With becoming an adult came the realization that there were no stickers and stars for me! With my government job came an annual performance review. The bottom-line was that, *'Once a year I will tell you if I like you. The rest of the time if I change my mind, I will let you know!'* That's also not right!

As an occupational health nurse, I have read many studies of what motivates people in the workplace. Most of them come to a similar conclusion: the thing that workers rank as most important to them is 'appreciation'. We crave being appreciated! (By the way, number two is 'feeling in on things', and number three is 'an understanding attitude'. Number four is 'job security'. Number five is 'fair wages'. A poster of this Top 10 list can be printed from my website: www.healthservsask.com)

When I started HEALTHSERV in 1992, and acquired staff as we grew, I worried that my employees would not be motivated nor be happy, as I could not pay top wages. When reading the results of a study about what motivates workers, I learned that they will stay or leave on the basis of whether more important values – apart from money – were present or not. I knew that I needed to create a workplace where people were appreciated, had a sense of belonging, and felt in on things. I committed to being an 'Encourager'.

These two ideas will help you do the same, and hope they may change your life, as they have changed mine. Commit to being an 'Encourager' in order to meet that most basic of needs in people – to be appreciated. These 2 ideas – 'Encouragement-Mail' and an 'Encouragement-File' – will help.

Encouragement Mail

While sitting in my bank manager's office one day, waiting for her to return, I was busy looking at her bulletin board. I love looking at bulletin boards! Bulletin boards are the occupational health nurse's method of taking the blood pressure of an organization – they give clues about the values, beliefs, and activities of that workplace. On her bulletin board, I saw all these little green notes with a cartoon fellow holding up his thumb and the slogan, 'You made the difference'. When she returned, I asked about those notes. "Oh, those are encouragement notes from co-workers. With everyone working flex-time, part-time, and Saturdays, it's so hard to get everyone together for a meeting, let alone a birthday party, so our manager instituted this idea of 'encouragement notes'. When we catch someone doing something well, we send a note of encouragement."

"You really all do this?" I remarked, almost not believing something so simple would be happening in this stiff corporate world. "Oh, yes! Some people do it more, and some people less. Our manager spends the first 20 minutes of each day

writing out encouragement notes from the day before." I contemplated the effect this idea would have on workplace morale, and I became excited! I was still curious, "What are the round pink notes?" "Oh," she remarked, her eyes twinkling, and her voice lowering, "those are from the boss!"

Wow! Imagine what you would do if you came into your office in the morning, and you saw a pink round note on your desk. You knew it would be something positive from your supervisor. Would you hang up your coat, check your e-mail, put your lunch in the fridge, get a cup of coffee, and check the lottery numbers from yesterday first? I don't think so! You would rip that little note open, and savour it – then, maybe post it on your bulletin board!

Since that memorable event at my bank, I have shared this idea with workplaces and groups all over who are struggling with the same issues of morale, team spirit, and how to stay connected. I now have an extensive collection of 'Corporate Encouragement Mail' ideas from all sorts of workplaces. Here are some of the best:

- A nursing home copied ghost shapes during the Halloween season with the phrase, 'You did a boooo-tiful job' written across the front for staff, volunteers, and family to use.
- One government office thought this idea might aid their morale, so they printed up little cards which said, 'You Done Good' for everyone to use. Since they handle very tough and draining cases, it was hard for staff to stay cheerful. I saw the manager several months later at a conference, and asked how the 'Encouragement-Mail' idea was going. *"Oh,"* she said. *"one of the sourpusses was quick to point out that our slogan was bad grammar. But, that same person has all her little cards she's received lined up across the front of her desk."*
- With volunteers, remember that your 'Encouragement Mail', such as a sincere, written thank- you, is all they get!
- A hospital was proud to show me their 'Tree of Thanks'. It was originally assembled in the dining room during the Thanksgiving season so staff, family, and volunteers could write notes of thanks on coloured leaves to fill up the tree. By the time I saw it, it had been 'transplanted' into the staff room across one wall, onto the ceiling, and around one corner because it was "too precious to throw in the garbage, so we just keep adding to it".

Life is short – never miss an opportunity to send a lovely handwritten note in the mail expressing your praise and delight at an accomplishment, promotion, picture in the paper, nomination or award. In our busy electronic world, the sentiment of a written note will stand out and be cherished. I can't tell you how many times I have sent someone a note to say *'Good for you!'* and they've told me I was the only one who wrote! What is remarkable about that is, not that I was so clever, but that I was the only one!

Encouragement File

If you really do reap what you sow, you will end up with lots of your own 'E-Mail' Where will you keep it all? I have an idea for you! Put all of your 'Encouragement Mail' into a special folder. (Some of you may be already using a shoe box – I guess that would make it an 'E-Box'!) My folder is labeled 'Arlene's Encouragement File', and is full of all kinds of lovely stuff: thank-you notes, congratulation letters, cards from flowers, jokes sent to me, news clippings that mention me or my business, and pictures that my little kids drew for me.

Now, on a good day, I don't need to look in there. But on a bad day, when I am feeling like the 'schmuck of the earth', and nothing is turning out right, I close the door and go through my 'E-Files'. Those encouraging notes, and the praise and compliments that were sincerely written to me, are the truth about who I am! They counteract how I am beating up on myself. Human nature is such that it is much easier for us to collect negative messages and replay them in our minds than for us to replay the good ones. That's why you and I need an 'E-file', to help us keep us in perspective.

For those of you with children, or who work with youth, teaching them to have a file like this is a must. The world is very quick to point out to young people that they are not tall enough, shapely enough, slim enough, cute enough, smart enough, popular enough, and on, and on, and on. It's not right.

Final Words from an 'Encourager'

You've just read about this nurse's ABC's for energy saving. It is critical that we check our attitudes daily, and be aware of gripping life more lightly, not more tightly. It makes you more fun to be around, and you'll live longer. Wouldn't you rather have lines from laughing, than from worrying?

Fix your brakes, not your accelerator. It's easier on your 'engine', and you'll enjoy the scenery much more. Commit yourself to being an Encourager – for others and yourself. Start by adopting one easy idea that will feed others' basic needs to be appreciated, and one idea to help your keep up your own morale.

Through these ABC's, my intent has been to inspire you to make an even stronger commitment to your own health and wellness, so that you are truly enjoying the time of your life. Remember to:

Stay cool when your pants are on fire!

Biography for Arlene Jorgenson

Business Name: HEALTHSERV
(Saskatchewan)
Address: 131 Wall Street,
Saskatoon, Saskatchewan
S7K 6C2
Telephone: (306) 374-9079
Fax: (306) 374-7246
Email: ajorgenson@healthservsask.com
Web Address: www.healthservsask.com

Canadian Association of Professional Speakers Chapter:
Saskatchewan, Professional member

About Arlene:
Arlene helps people live and work with more health, fun and passion. She is a businesswoman with a degree in nursing from the University of Saskatchewan, and a specialty designation in occupational health nursing from the Canadian Nurses Association. She is the founder and owner of HEALTHSERV since 1992, the largest occupational health consulting company in the province with clinics in Regina and Saskatoon that specialize in substance abuse prevention programs, independent medicals and hearing conservation.

Arlene won the North Saskatoon Business Builder award for innovation in 2001, and a finalist for the Saskatoon Chamber of Commerce Business Excellence award in 2001. Her client list includes Weyerhaeuser Canada, Hitachi Canada, Government of Saskatchewan, IPSCO, BASF, and Husky Oil.

Arlene is an experienced and capable healer. It is her enthusiastic devotion to personal empowerment and belief in 'laughter as the best medicine' that enables her to cure the ailing spirit that is experienced by many today. Her most popular keynote presentations are: *'Thankfully, I had a Tractor'* (to fuel the entrepreneurial spirit) and *'How to Stay Cool when Your Pants are on Fire'* (boosting morale at work and home). Arlene's most popular seminars are *'Powerful Presentation Skills for Leadership Success'*, *'Substance Abuse Prevention Training for Supervisors'*, *'Hearing Conservation Program Management for OH&S Managers'*, and *'Audiometric Technician's Course.'*

"Live and work but do not forget to play,
to have fun in life and really enjoy it."

- Eileen Caddy

Take Your Health to Higher Heights

By: Natalie J. Forstbauer
dare2feel Training and Development International

Love your body, and it will produce miracles for you.

The first time I put gas in a car, it was lonely and embarrassing. It was a hot summer afternoon. The sun was beating down on me, and the gas gauge was reading below empty. There was no escape from fuelling up. The gas station was buzzing with people. The pump was an overwhelming sight to my virgin eyes. Up until that moment, my experience at the gas station was sitting in the vehicle, while my Mom fuelled up. Mystified and dumbfounded, I stood gawking, wondering where to begin. There were no instructions! At 16 years old, in my panic to be 'cool', I grabbed for what I thought might be the nozzle. The hose seemed to have so many places where it began and ended. Strings were attached to it, and handles were protruding from everywhere. To make matters worse, there was more than one type of gas to choose from!

> *We want to be healthy and make healthy choices, but how do we make the right choices?*

I could not believe my Mom did not give me a lesson before sending me to get gas, or at least have given me a quick "this is how to pump gas" once-over. My fragile ego would have been thankful. I finally found the end of the hose where I was pretty certain the gas would flow from. Now, if I could only find the magic button to make the gas come out. After what seemed to be hours of inner dialogue, struggle, and strife, I found the lever to push down, and make the gas flow. Whew! What an ordeal.

In North America, shopping for food can be like my first experience pumping gas. We go to a grocery store and we are inundated – sometimes even overwhelmed – by countless numbers of products. They are geared to win us over and make us buy, buy, buy. Like me figuring out how to pump gas, how do we know where to begin? How do we know what to buy and what not to buy? It seems we want to be healthy, and make healthy choices, but with all the propaganda, how do we make the right choice? My goal in this chapter is to give you tools to take your health to higher heights. We will explore where to begin, what it takes to cultivate a healthy lifestyle, and discover ways to make your health a priority. You will have the opportunity to define what health means to you, and what you need to do to have a balanced and 'health-full' life.

Change Your Oil Regularly

Imagine you are given one vehicle for life. Given this vehicle must last you your entire life, how would you treat it? How often would you change the oil? What grade fuel would you use? How often would you tune it up – or would you bother? How often would it get washed? Knowing this vehicle had to last you a lifetime, *how would you treat it?* Now, imagine yourself standing naked in front of a mirror. Take a good look at the reflection. This is your vehicle for life. You were born with it. It is yours to keep and look after.

Raised on a BioDynamic Certified Organic Vegetable and Blueberry farm, you might think I would be the last to be diagnosed with Chronic Fatigue Syndrome (CFS) and Fybromyalgia. This was not so. In 1990, I was in a car accident that left me with a lower back injury, whiplash, and a concussion. Eventually, I had little to no use of my right arm. Unfortunately – or fortunately – it took being diagnosed with the symptoms of CFS and Fybromyalgia before I regained my health. It was through my recovery, and quest for health, that I discovered we have one vehicle for life. I learned to value, respect and honour it.

Eat for Energy (NRG)

Eat for Nourishment, Rejuvenation, and Growth (NRG). Your energy level is only as good as the fuel you have to burn. Knowing you have one vehicle for life, what type of fuel do you choose to consume? It is easy in a go-go-go society to eat on the run, drink on the run, and shop on the run. To make things even easier, everything is in nice little packages and bars for us to consume easily, and effortlessly. Packaged food is engineered to give optimal nutrition and value. It is brilliant! The challenge is: packaged food is also full of additives, chemicals, sugar, and preservatives. Research is now questioning the safety of these additives, and how they are contributing to diseases, including cancer. The other downside of eating packaged foods is people are losing touch with the source of their food, and the value in eating real, living food.

Real, living food, consists of fresh fruits, vegetables, sprouts and legumes. Certified Organic or BioDynamic foods are your best choice when shopping for optimal health and vitality. Buying Certified Organic is worth it! The bonus items in conventional foods include chemicals, pesticides, fungicides, and herbicides. Some conventional foods are even bleached and go through radiation – yes, radiation – to increase their shelf life. Some of the most common vegetables, such as corn and cauliflower, are bleached a minimum of one time before they reach the consumer. I almost fell over when I learned corn is bleached, after it is blanched, before it reaches the freezer. It amazes me how we – the consumer – are unaware of how our food is grown and treated before it reaches our body.

Chemicals, herbicides, and fungicides are used to kill bugs, weeds, and diseases. They are absorbed by the foods we eat. Unfortunately, we are uncertain of the long-term effects of these practices on us humans at the end of the food chain. Research is showing that they, too, are believed to be harmful. The value in eating Certified Organic or BioDynamic produce is that it goes through an inspection process to ensure none of these harmful chemicals are used. Certified Organic and BioDynamic farmers have their farms and records inspected regularly. Ponder this: we could continue as we are, and perhaps, we won't have to embalm future generations, thanks to all the preservatives in our diet now.

Shop at organic specialty stores and farmer's markets. Begin a community garden or order from an organic home delivery company. In the average grocery store, food is often two weeks old by the time it reaches your fridge. As soon as the food has been picked, it begins to lose its nutritional value. Shopping at alternative locations increases the nutritional value of your food.

Listening to your Body's Intelligence

The clue to knowing what foods are best for your body is paying attention to your body's intelligence. Our bodies have a blue print to perfect health. The body knows exactly what it needs to obtain and sustain optimal health. We need to listen to what our bodies tell us, notice how we feel when we eat different foods, and see how our bodies respond to what we consume.

Many people watch for little signs that tell them if something is good or less than good for their bodies. Here are some common signs that food is harmful: a rush of saliva in the mouth as food touches the tongue, cramping in the tummy, bloating, gas, fatigue, anxiety, hot flashes, cold chills, headaches, heartburn, or a metallic taste in the mouth. There are more signs, and I am sure you have noticed some of them. The key is to do something about them. For example, stop eating these foods. After eating healthy, live foods, people notice how great they feel. Their stomach feels consistently flat, they are content, and they get energy (NRG) from the foods they eat. You can even train your senses to tell you or show you what foods are best for you.

Food-testing exercise: The exercise is quite simple. It just takes some practice. When shopping for your food, hold the feeling, vision, and intention of complete, total, optimal health. Before you put an item in your cart, hold it in your hand. Ask yourself, "Does this give me optimal health?" You will get a 'yes', or 'no' answer. *Yes* will be for, "Yes, this food is great for my health", and *No* will be for "No, I need to choose something better for my health". Everyone experiences 'yes' and 'no' differently. Some people hear the 'yes' or 'no' in their heads, others get a feeling of 'yes' or 'no' and, for some, the 'yes' and 'no' have to make sense. However you get your 'yes' and 'no' is perfectly fine.

Another thing to notice is cravings. If you are craving certain vegetables, chances are your body needs them. If you are craving sugars, breads, coffee, sweets, and chocolate, chances are your body is addicted to them. As you become more conscious of foods that create health for your body, you will have fewer cravings for harmful foods, and more cravings towards foods that are good for you. You will notice that when you eat well, you have energy to put into having the work-life balance you deserve and desire.

Eating habits are integral in creating a healthy environment for your body to flourish. Here are some tips to maximize the nutrition you absorb from the foods you eat. Savour and taste the food as it greets your palate. Fully chew your food 20-30 times before swallowing it. Before you put a new mouthful of food into your mouth, completely swallow your previous mouthful. Eat in silence, honouring your body's innate intelligence to absorb the NRG (Nutrition, Regeneration, and Growth) from the food you eat. Pay attention to your body's messages, respecting its requests and wishes.

Flush Your Toilet!

Great, now that you have the tools you need to eat well, imagine not flushing your toilet for a whole day, or even a couple of days. Gross, right? Disgusting – yes! Well, we need to flush our inner plumbing system often. Imagine not watering a plant for a long time. It dries out the soil. The first time you water the plant, the water runs right through the soil, sometimes creating a mess!

Have you ever noticed your body gets stiff part way through the day? Or perhaps you wake up a bit stiff in the mornings? Or maybe you get headaches throughout the day, or more in the afternoon. Maybe you get tired as the day goes on, or you become slightly irritable and edgy? These symptoms can be directly related to dehydration. When babies are born, they are said to be at the optimal level of fluid for their bodies – 85% hydrated. An elderly person is merely 15% hydrated. Your body needs water!

Some people feel drinking water makes them visit the restroom more often. The first time you oil your pipes, you may be running to the washroom a lot, but think about it, you have a lot of waste to get rid of! Not drinking adequate amounts of water is like not flushing your toilet for an extended period of time. Your body has a hard time cleaning up after itself when it is dehydrated. Drinking eight glasses of water a day is like keeping your toilet bowl clean. Once your body has reached equilibrium, it will be easier to maintain a healthy hydration level. If you are thirsty, you are already 10% dehydrated.

A simple glass of water can actually take the edge off. Put a water jug in your office. Notice how much it is used, and how pleasant your co-workers and staff become. One of my clients did this, and it worked! Not only were people more pleasant at work when the water was introduced to their department, but there was a greater sense of community. It is amazing what a little bit of good old-fashioned water does! Keep your body fresh, and refreshed. Remember to flush your toilet!

Purified water, distilled water, reversed osmosis water, spring water, tap water… which is the best water to drink? Great question! There is a lot of debate on this subject. Here are a couple of different thoughts. Firstly, tap water is contaminated with chlorine bleach and sometimes fluoride. Chlorine is hard on your system.

> *"Drinking chlorinated water may as much as double the risk of bladder cancer."*
> *- Kenneth Cantor, National Cancer Institute*

Fluoride in tap water is a growing concern too. In July of 1997, NFFE (National Federation of Federal Employees) stated:

> *Our review of evidence from the last 11 years, including human studies, indicates a causal link between fluoride and cancer, genetic damage, and neurological impairment. Of particular concern are studies linking fluoride exposure to lowered IQ in children.*

In the same breath, drinking tap water is better than drinking no water. It is important to drink filtered or purified water, and a *reversed osmosis* filtering system for water is one of the best types. Here is a helpful option if you only have access to tap water: Pour a jug of water and let it sit on the counter for a few hours. In this time, I find the chlorine evaporates from the water. It is easier to drink. You can also boil it first. Get used to drinking water. Make it a priority, and notice the difference it makes in your life.

Health is a Habit

Health is a learned state and condition. When my doctor was diagnosing me with CFS and Fybromyalgia, he explained to me that because it was taking so long for me to heal from the car accident, the pain, fatigue, headaches and discomfort I was experiencing were becoming learned conditions. My body was getting so used to being in pain, discomfort, and out of balance, that it was slowly becoming its regular state of being. My body was literally learning to look for – and recognize – pain. Hmmmmmm…I thought, *"If my body can learn to be in pain, it can learn to not be in pain. It can learn to be healthy."* My doctor agreed.

In truth, the greatest key that moved me forward beyond CFS and Fibromyalgia was my relearning to be healthy. I taught my body to respond healthily to eating live, healthy foods, encouraged my body to love the taste of water, and made my health a priority.

The body has an innate intelligence, and a blueprint to perfect health. It needs to be nurtured and loved. It needs to be taught, and guided. It is like a vehicle that needs a driver to show it where to go, and how to get to its destination. Grab hold of your wheel, see where you are going, tune into being healthy, and be the driver.

It is interesting that many conversations revolve around what is wrong in life, and how sick, or ill people are. These discussions actually reinforce negativity and poor health. Practicing the habit of health includes healthy dialogue. Engage in healthy conversations. Talk about where to get the best and healthiest foods, how great things are going, and what is going 'right' in your life.

Health is a state of being that needs to be practiced. Even the top athletes and performers in the world practice their art to be the best. Put your focus on being healthy. Practice healthy habits. The following exercise will help. Make a list. _____'s *(your name) daily healthy habits are*: (list 5 daily healthy habits).

1. _____

2. _____

3. _____

4. _____

5. _____

Begin with one healthy habit a day. Every 21 days, add a new habit, until you are practicing five healthy habits a day, consistently.

Your Bottom Line Depends on Your Health

How often have you walked into a store where the clerk or sales person was in a bad mood, or in poor health, and she/he complained about it? When they have complained about their frustrations, didn't you question doing business with them, or doing business again with them? This behavior, and state of mind, can be quite toxic – draining, in fact! It is like the life-blood is being vacuumed out of you. I call these people 'energy-suckers'. They are predators feasting on negative vibes, basking in the mediocrity of their life. Wouldn't it be great to be on the receiving end of someone who was at the other end of that pendulum, spilling over with vitality and healthy energy?

Our family farm spends a great deal of time serving the public at farmer's markets, and doing off-the-farm sales. We also participate in trades shows and various other educational/volunteer projects, working directly with customers. In working with my younger siblings, I have had the pleasure of mentoring them in 'Customer Service 101'. The first principle they learn is to engage, and embrace, in a healthy state. A healthy state goes beyond a smile and a healthy body. It reaches into the mind, body and soul, touching people emotionally, mentally, physically, and spiritually. Health is a state of being. It is something that is expressed through thoughts, actions, words, and poise. A healthy spirit and mind results in a healthy body.

When you exude rich energy full of health and vitality, it enrolls people to be around you and do business with you. Your healthy, vibrant state releases pheromones into the air. The pheromones make people feel good, and in turn, cause them to want to come back and do business with you. It leaves them with a good feeling; something they cannot quite put their finger on, but nonetheless, it is a good feeling that they remember. The memory becomes something they relate to you. When they think of your product, or use your product they are anchored to their experience of your 'healthy state', which resonates within them. How refreshing is it be greeted by someone who is vibrant, full of energy, and radiating health? These people are like magnets, aren't they? People hunger to be around happy and healthy people.

Engage yourself in a healthy state with your mind, body, and soul. Be passionate about what you share with your co-workers, clients, customers, company, staff, and boss. Notice your thoughts, and make them work for you. Look for and find reasons to be healthy, to be happy and to be engaged in life. People are drawn to that energy. They yearn to be a part of it, and have a taste of it.

The Beauty of Balance

What is important to you? What *juices* you and gets you excited? What makes you feel alive inside? What gives you inner peace? What do you feel good about spending time on and doing? What makes you healthy and balanced?

A colleague and great friend of mine who owns a very successful business has dedicated the last seven years of her life to building her business empire. In her first few years of business, she found balance in spending a large part of her time marketing her business, and less time socializing. To her, balance was spending longer hours at work, a few hours exercising, and a night or two of socializing a week. Now, seven years later, her definition of balance has changed. Balance is now spending less time in her business, spending more time with her friends and family, and doing recreational activities. Sometimes, people romanticize balance and ask what it 'should be'. I ask: "What do you want, and desire it to be?"

Once in a while, I put my life balance to the test. One summer, I thought I could manage my business and my parent's farm successfully. It was a challenge getting there! The biggest obstacle was taking on too much. Does that ever happen to you? I call it ICDE [pronounced ick-day] Syndrome. I Can Do Everything Syndrome! I CAN return phone calls on time, submit proposals, market new projects, write articles, write my book, manage the blueberry fields, do my business payroll, pay the pickers, start new projects, and take care of all the details in between – not just some, but ALL of the details in between! Typical of an over-achiever, isn't it? It took me about a week to recognize that I had over committed myself, and another week to get back into balance.

Do you ever notice how drained, worn thin, and out of balance you feel when you are over committed or have lost your sense of balance? Stress felt from being out of balance contributes to poor health. That summer, I took a time out to re-evaluate what balance was to *me,* and what I needed to do to be balanced.

Going Inside Yourself

A person's state of health is a picture of what is going on internally for them. The work-life balance you strive for will naturally fall into place as you define what balance means to you. Your health will innately improve as you have less stress in your life, and you are more in balance.

A good place to start defining balance is through going inside. Do an internal check on what moves and balances you. You can define balance by asking yourself a series of questions. These questions let you know your value system, and align you with what is important. Through spending time answering the questions, you'll gain a good idea of what makes sense in your life, and also what you need to do to live in a balanced way.

Use this series of questions, and the space following, to help you define and understand what balance means to you, and what you need to do to live in balance:

- What does balance mean to me?
- If I had balance, how would I know I had it?
- What do I need to do to have balance in my life?
- What will propel me forward to living in balance, now?
- What will I do now to live the balanced life I deserve and desire?

_____

_____

_____

_____

_____

_____

I used this set of questions to regain balance in my life when I was over committed to my business and blueberry fields. The answers derived from the questions are powerful. I encourage you to implement the answers revealed to you.

Be Engaged in Your Health

Where is your health now, and where do you want it to be? What will you take away from this chapter, and implement in your life today? Perhaps it is eating food that will give you NRG, flushing your toilet, maximizing the nutrition from the food you eat, practicing your daily health habits, or creating more balance in your life. Whatever you decide to do, always be engaged in your health. Embrace and live being healthy. Surround yourself with healthy people, and be excited about your health. Where you are right now is perfect. You will do what you need to do, and be where you need to be. Trust that, and be committed to it. There are days when all I want to do is eat chocolate, but, thankfully, those days pass. Every day I learn more about what I need to do to take my health to higher heights, and I am sure you do too. Health is a habit that needs to be practiced daily.

Remember to love your body, and it will produce miracles for you!

Biography for Natalie J. Forstbauer

Business Name: dare2feel Training and
Development International
Address: 7496 Gibson Road,
Chilliwack, British Columbia
V2R 1B1
Telephone: (877) 559-3273
Email: natalie@dare2feel.com
Web Address: www.dare2feel.com

Canadian Association of Professional Speakers Chapter:
British Columbia, Professional Member

About Natalie:
Natalie Forstbauer, is more than just a speaker – people find her charisma and passion for life contagious. She specializes in helping people cultivate health and work-life balance by exploring, seeding and discovering the body's innate intelligence to be healthy.

She is a Consultant, Coach and Certified Polarity Therapist known as radio personality "Dr. Feel Good" who charms her listeners with wit and wisdom by sharing healthy, relaxing, and rejuvenating tips to lead a full and balanced life. She beat Fibromyalgia and Chronic Fatigue Syndrome through all natural means. Natalie is a corporate founder of the number one positive news website: www.newsforthesoul.com. A columnist for Mind, Body, Soul Magazine, she answers workplace wellness questions in her *'Essence of the Workplace'* segment.

Online Resources by Natalie:
E-Courses: 101 Healthy Habits, 365 Days of Inspiration, 7 Secrets to Balance, Weekly/Daily Neck and Shoulder Revitalizers, Foodtrition and Herbtrition

Zenergy Membership: Discover ways to naturally improve your work-life balance, health and wellness. Your Zenergy membership includes: streaming videos, e-classes, and health e-tools to relax, rejuvenate, and relieve stress.

"No one can make you feel inferior without your consent."
- Eleanor Roosevelt

Fly Like An Eagle

By: Joan Kulmala
Totally-U Image Communications

Find, connect and discover how to fly through life like an eagle.

Realizing the impact and importance of creating a positive image is critical for women in today's fast paced world. The image that you project is there for the entire world to see. Through this chapter, you will learn to equate the image of an eagle to your personal image. All you need to do is recognize that change is possible, and you can have a more powerful, dynamic image like the eagle.

Each afternoon, as I sat on my son's deck in beautiful Victoria, British Columbia, a pair of bald eagles would appear, soaring majestically over towering trees in the distance. I marveled at their power, grace, strength, agility, and the freedom that they were experiencing. They appeared not to have a care in the world. Of course once I really looked, I discovered that there was a deeper substance to these majestic birds than met the naked eye. I realized they were on a mission. This ritual of scanning the landscape below them was a necessary part of their daily routine. There was courage, power, grace, focus, tenacity, patience, and beauty soaring high in the sky. This made me feel empowered as I realized my connection with the eagle. Through this chapter, you can realize your connection too!

Do You Know Who You Are?

Upon sighting the eagle in flight, I immediately jumped to conclusions. This huge bird was quite intimidating and frightening, to say the least. When I took the time to really look for other attributes, I realized that this was a creature of substance and purpose. People come in all sizes: tall, short, thin or full-figured. One cannot assume the level of fitness or wellness of another person simply by looks alone. Similar to the eagle, each of us is endowed with many characteristics that will assist us in taking flight, no matter what phase of our journey we have reached.

Making the Transition

Some things cannot be changed, such as your parents, the colour of your skin, the size of your hands or feet – but, there are many things that can. After recognizing the need to alter your flight, you (and only you) must make the decision to take action.

As you pass through life, you will experience many changes, both professionally and personally. Changes happen for a variety of reasons. A shift in your health status, family challenges, or career changes are only a few reasons why we are forced to make adjustments. For many of us, there have been and will continue to be variable circumstances that will definitely alter the course that we take. As I think back to my own course of life travel, I have ventured down many paths.

My trip through life has been quite diversified. I have been a nurse, a sales person – selling everything from fashion textiles to granite monuments – an aquatics instructor, a member of the naval reserve, and currently, an entrepreneur. It was through each of these experiences that I learned to be flexible in my thoughts, and in my actions. Often, it meant facing the reality of the situation, and coming to terms with the issues before me.

One prime example was when my doctor told me that I needed to give up nursing, after spending 20 years in the profession. Prior to having major back surgery, then falling off a chair, fracturing my spine, and spending five years confined to a bed, life was good. As fate would have it, I was forced to go through a metamorphosis. At that critical point in my life, I came to the conclusion that I had two choices. I could either take to my bed, and become a non-productive individual with a bleak future or, I could rethink my positioning. Not one to lie down and die, I chose to look for new horizons. Many friends have asked me if my middle name was 'Pollyanna'. Having a positive disposition, I have always been able to look at things with optimism and hope. I carry 'Plan B' in my pocket at all times.

As I had a permanent disability, how was I going to adapt? Having time to be creative, I explored a variety of new possibilities by taking the time to brainstorm other options. This was a very intense time of self-discovery. Thus, I was able to channel my path to a new career. Having completed this process, I was surprised to discover that I had many skills, qualities, and strengths on which to build. I found that my strengths far outweighed my weaknesses. This was a starting point for me, and I have never looked back. I recommend this

> *I found that my strengths far outweighed my weaknesses.*
> *I never looked back.*

course of self-discovery for anyone questioning her self-worth. Each of us is unique, with hidden resources just waiting to be discovered and put to good use. The following is an exercise to assist you, and you can use the space below to record your results:

Part #1: Take a few moments to make a written list of your strengths and weaknesses. Remember, you will probably be more critical of yourself than others. The key is to be brutally honest with yourself. No matter how insignificant you think your strengths or weaknesses are, write them down.

Part #2: Now, look at the list. Most likely, you will note, as I did, that your strengths list outweighed your weaknesses. How did you rate? Once you have completed this simple exercise, I trust that you will make discoveries similar to my own.

Part #3: How do you build upon your strengths, and what changes need to be addressed at this time? Prioritize your lists and then go to work. Keep your flight at a minimum. Soar slowly, and evenly. This should help to make your transition easier. Remember, it has taken you many years to get into your current position. You cannot expect change will happen overnight. As you look over your written words, you will find that they have more weight than with simply thinking about them. Visually, you can see the power of who you are, just as the eagle soars high above, and is able to zone in on the littlest creatures far below.

_____

_____

_____

_____

_____

_____

Stepping Out of Your Comfort Zone

Few will find it easy to make this transition from one phase of their lives to another, while others will encounter a heightened level of stress and difficulty. It is during this period that you will have to step out of your comfort zone to take action. Yes, it is risky, but change often opens doors to many new and exciting things. Change is never easy. It is work. Do not think that it just happens. You have the capabilities and tools to shape your own destiny, but you must be willing to exert some energy, and have the desire to assume the position to fly. In order to get on with living a productive life again, you must face reality. Consider this as your opportunity to acquire what you will need to soar. Where do you start?

Assistance with Stepping Out of Your Comfort Zone
First Step: Have you ever said any of the following to yourself?

- Why me?
- How will I survive?
- It's not fair!
- I can't go on.

This is a natural process. I call it the mourning period, and it's OK to grieve first in order to make the transition.

Reaction: You need to verbally ventilate, cry, take time out, sleep, or mope. (I certainly did my share of grieving). Oftentimes, I felt completely out of control with no self-esteem. Fear of the unknown crept inside my stomach. Feelings of worthlessness and inadequacy as a wife, mother, and productive individual nagged at me constantly. The song 'Cry Me a River' certainly became my swan song during that time.

Action: Stop, Think, and Take Some Deep Breaths!
Do what you must to get your frustrations out. Exercise, clean the house, punch a pillow, or run a marathon, but let your anxiety out. Come to terms with making modifications in your life. Here are some suggestions:

- Be prepared to take a risk, and step out of your comfort zone.
- Be creative by digging deep within yourself to discover new ideas and innovative ways to make a positive transition.
- Use the process of brainstorming. I love this exercise. It's great to be the creator and beneficiary of new ideas.
- Seek the support of your family, friends, and co-workers.
- Each day, take time out for you. Pamper yourself.

One way or the other, a person must be prepared to face reality and initiate the necessary action. The feathers of an eagle are lightweight but strong, hollow but pliable. Their prime purpose is to protect the birds from the changeable climates into which they fly. Are you prepared to take flight?

What I saw in the Eagle

Courage

It takes inner resolve and peace with oneself to meet challenges head on. Set your goals so that they are personally attainable by drawing from your life's work. It may be as simple as re-evaluating where you have come from, where you wish to go, what do you want to do, and how do you get there? Do you want to roll over and fall off the face of the earth? At this point, are you able to find the courage to take control in order to make the positive choices which will allow the eagle in you to soar?

Power

The dictionary defines power as *'the ability to act; particular faculty of body or mind; vigour, energy'.* Each of you has the power to grow, and learn from past mistakes and experiences. It is all in how you handle it! If you realize that you need to feel good inside before you will have the strength to create a positive outer image, you will survive.

Think back to when you were a child - how much power did you have? In my era, my parents made all the choices for me. By gradually bestowing responsibilities upon me at various milestones in my life, I was taught how life worked. With each choice one makes, accountability and responsibilities follow. I'm sure you can relate to this.

Power and strength is an inner resolve. It is spiritual. You have to feel it, and have a firm desire to take control, and only you can take charge. All the expert advice and consultations with professionals will not be the only determining factors of how you will proceed. It's like the old saying, *"You can take a horse to water, but you cannot make it drink."* With each day, an eagle gains strength and power as it attends to its daily tasks. You can, too!

Grace

In today's society, people are so busy with careers and family. Often, the simple art of 'social graces' gets lost. I have always been a believer in treating others as I would like to be treated myself. Never losing sight of this simple belief, I am at peace at the end of the day, knowing that I have treated others with dignity and respect.

As a facilitator, I often start my Image presentation by asking one simple question. *"What time do you set your radio alarm clock to rise in the morning?"* Many individuals will respond with on the hour or half hour, while a few will state that they set it five to ten minutes before the hour or half hour. Which is better? The latter is the optimal choice. Ask yourself 'what comes on the radio on the hour or half hour?' If you responded 'the news', you are right. And, what is the first thing that is reported? Ninety-nine point nine percent of it is doom and gloom. On the other hand if your alarm is set earlier, it will certainly be music. Music is positive, and it undoubtedly will have a positive impact on setting the tone for the start of your day. Chances are, this graceful start to your morning will carry well into the remainder of your day. Occasionally, I find myself humming at the end of the workday, the tune I heard at five to the hour in the morning. Which would you rather wake up to?

Presence

A positive outward appearance is often linked to having a sense of well-being. Your level of self-confidence is revealed through your personality with every experience in your life, whether it is positive or negative. It is human nature for you to be influenced by what you see. Consequently, at that time, conclusions are drawn. Your presence can be felt by others. Often, one can pick up on such things as the level of energy you are exhibiting, and even the frame of mind you are in – be it happy or sad. The challenge is for you to seek out a tiny ray of light, and prepare yourself to dust off the ruffled feathers, in order to fly again.

It is amazing how resilient people are. Just think of some of the negative things that you have gone through. Perhaps it's the loss of a loved one, loss of a job, deteriorating health, or loss of financial stability that you can relate to. Now, think of some positive things that you have experienced: scholastic achievements, new birth, achieving personal goals, etc. How did each of these experiences make you feel? How did you handle them? What did you learn from the experience? How were you able to get on with your life?

Negative experiences often leave one drained with no enthusiasm, lack of energy, low self-esteem, and a detrimental affect on your physical well-being. On the other hand, positive experiences leave you with enthusiasm, an elevated energy level, and allow you to become one with your inner and outer self. By simulating yourself to be like an eagle, you can radiate confidence and competence to others, as you take flight to your future.

> **It is only through experiencing and living through the ups and downs of life's trials and tribulations that your outer confidence will have been unveiled.**

The female bald eagle certainly has presence. She is slightly larger than the male. Her wingspan varies adding to her greatness. As one sights this magnificent bird in flight, one cannot help but feel her presence. It is not an intimidating presence, but an awesome sight as she takes command, and glides effortlessly through the air. Once the eagle in you is ready to climb with presence, others will be inspired to follow. You can become a role model to those aspiring to spread their wings.

Focus

Have a dream, follow it, mold it, and never lose sight of where you have been, or where you are going. Consider past experiences as your personal school of learning. Look at them as adventures, not impositions. Once an eagle has taken flight, she can soar hundreds of feet above the earth. By focusing on the terrain far below her, she is able to spot the smallest animal, and then zoom in for the catch from that great height. With intense concentration in her eyes, she never loses sight of her prey. As you focus upon your horizon, do it with a deep passion, sincere belief, and love so intense that you can actually breathe it, feel it, and taste it. Enjoy the journey – it will not be boring. On the contrary, you are guaranteed to experience a renewed intensity of being!

Tenacity

The image that we build for ourselves starts when we are in our early stages of life. As a child, I would often question and balk at the simplest of lesson my parents would try to teach me. I could not see the rationale for their antiquated ideas. Basic responsibilities of contributing to the running of our household: doing chores, learning the value of honesty, independence, and integrity were just a few of the lessons that I was faced with as a young person growing up in the 50's. To this date, I still hold strong to those principles that I learned so many years ago. At the end of each day, I am able to rest knowing that I have faced the day with tenacity. I think it must be the eagle in me that inspires me to think this way. I invite you to seek the eagle in you. Once you have found her, she will motivate you.

Patience

In today's fast paced world, people tend to want things immediately, or yesterday. Often, it is not possible for many individuals and organizations that have gone through some sort of restructuring to expect immediate change. People are instinctively creatures of habit. Any change made suddenly stirs up unwanted anxiety.

I remember walking into my exercise class when our instructor had the nerve to change the flow of our exercise program to go in the opposite direction. All participants were momentarily miffed. *"It feels different. I don't like this. Do we have to?"* These were only a few of the comments that were verbalized. Amazingly, once we got started working with the various machines, it did not take long to accept and enjoy the switch. Think of a time when you perhaps over-reacted and became impatient? How did you handle it? It's all a matter of taking control, a deep breath, and re-evaluating the situation. Later, upon reflection, you will find that things were not as bad as you thought. With a little patience, and a willingness to reassess the situation you will be able to come up with a viable solution. The old saying goes, *'patience is a virtue'* is still a valuable tool you can practise in your professional and personal life.

Beauty

Feeling good from within is the prerequisite to feeling good on the outside. People are intelligent – they can tell if you are faking it. The image that one creates for oneself must be slowly developed. It is that substructure of your being that will ultimately help you to address the image that you would like to create for yourself on the outside.

Looking Fabulous With What You Have

A starting point to address your exterior image is to accept yourself as you are. Looking fabulous with what you have is an attitude and it feels good. I have always been on the fuller figure side of the scale. I have often kidded with others that I was born at a hundred pounds, and my weight has always been a concern. Over the years, I have learned to deal with this.

Trying to obtain an unrealistic weight goal all but consumed me. I made it my mission to try every diet I could get my hands on. Nothing seemed to work. Athletically speaking, I was fit as a fiddle, until my spinal problems took over. Even then, I was able to function fairly well with a little modification to my daily routine.

After being seriously ill in the hospital, with my only sustenance being intravenous fluid for a period of 14 days, I decided to weigh myself. I was sure that I would have lost a great deal of weight. I could not believe my eyes, as the scale only registered *three itsy-bitsy pounds* lost. I did not even present a morsel of food to my lips in that period. Any other person would have lost at least 10 pounds! It was at that moment that I came to terms with what I looked like. Being a person with a deep sense of inner faith, I looked upward and knew that my God had blessed me. He said, *"Bless you Joan, this is who you are. Be happy."* From that day forth, I decided not to get stressed out about numbers and the smaller things in life, as long as I was able to maintain a comfortable level of health and wellness. If a diet and exercise routine is on your agenda, then do it wisely, with the help of your physician. People often strive to copy a certain look that they have seen on television or in magazines. BEWARE! That look may not be for you.

Repackaging Your Exterior

Appearance is your most tangible credential that radiates your level of competence and confidence. Start with a smile on your face. It takes fewer muscles to smile than it does to frown. As I get older, I believe that this action has helped keep some of the wrinkles away. Not to say that I have not earned my share…but it has helped. The expression on your face is within your control. Only you can adjust it! Try to discover – and use – a little humour. When things seem low, it will help to lift you up, and help you to regain prospective.

Similar to an eagle, you are uniquely beautiful.

A friend wrote the following piece. She has artistically painted a picture with prose, clarifying the correlation of a woman and an eagle:

IN EAGLE-MIND

I am the eagle.
I soar and play among the thermal drafts,
Master of the Air, that you can only breathe.
I drift among the high currents, above cathedral mountains
And look down upon the earth from a higher perspective.
My eyes, sharp and clear, see the panorama of miles in a glance
And yet, I see the smallest mouse that scampers under a leafy bower.

Do you envy my power?
I am creator-made for the air.
You are creator-made for the earth
We are each the perfection of what we are.
I am the eagle.

If you would dare to risk the ride on the not-solid air,
I can lead you to a high realm.
Feel the wind as it ruffles your hair, so it ruffles my feathers.
As the breeze caresses your face,
It will sing to you of the places it has been, as it sings to me.
Listen carefully.

Feel the air wrap under your body and lift you softly and then,
Feel the surge as it catches under your perfect wings
And you rise, Sacred Smoke from Sacred Fire
Spiraling, rising, higher and higher.
Here, where the air is thin and cold
Where the clouds billow and ebb and flow
Like ocean froth on the sea below
Here you are in eagle-mind.

No longer earthbound, you rest, wings spread wide
Borne upon the breath of god, you glide
All land laid out like a patchwork quilt for your eagle eyes.
All obstacles, once huge in human sight,
Melt away while in eagle's flight.
You are in eagle-mind.

Delight is yours as you dance on the shafts of sunlight
That split the morning clouds
And bring you toward a new dawn.
Life has no limits and you transcend.
You are in Eagle-Mind.

Author: D. Deprophetis

The Time has Come To fly Like an Eagle

The Image that you create for yourself has to be a total package. With every passing day, an eagle gains strength and poise. With each passing moment, she becomes one with herself and her surroundings. Learning to grow from your mistakes and experiences is never easy. Too often, people tend to zone in on the negatives in their lives, and many get stuck there, unable to see *'the pot of gold at the end of the rainbow'*. We are frequently judged on how we act before we say anything. Therefore, it is very important to be aware of the various messages that are transmitted through the image and habits that you develop and practice throughout your life. In order to fly like an eagle, you must take the time to recognize your own personal needs, dreams, and goals. When you are feeling low, and need a picker-upper, take a moment to visualize an eagle soaring high in the sky. See her courage, power, grace, focus, tenacity, patience and beauty. Enjoy the image you have fashioned for yourself – for THE EAGLE HAS LANDED within you. Now is your time to spread your wings and fly.

Biography for Joan Kulmala

Business Name: Totally-U Image
Communications
Address: 481 Dewe Avenue
Thunder Bay, Ontario
P7A 2G6
Telephone: (807) 683 8855
Fax: (807) 683 8855
Email: askjoan@totally-u.com
Web Address: www.totally-u.com

Canadian Association of Professional Speakers:
Professional Member

About Joan:
Joan inspires and motivates people to develop and hone their 'soft people skills'
for both professional and personal growth. A firm believer in feeling good from
within first, she invites others to radiate that feeling outwards. Both private and
corporate sectors continue to benefit from her motivational and inspiring
presentations. Clients are invited to *enjoy learning without pain* as she weaves a
mix of common sense and humour into her presentations.

Joan's accomplishments include various Chamber of Commerce awards,
Business Women's Network awards, and she produced, hosted and edited a six-
part series on image for public television. Clients include a variety of
organizations – Hydro One, hospitality, educational, business networks, health
services, government (WSIB), retail, tourism, and non-profit groups. She
continues to coach others through her writings for various newspapers and
magazines.

Joan empowers others to 'fly like an eagle' to be totally-you.

Shift Your Perception ...
Change Your Life!

By: Dawn Brown
Perception Shift

*Choosing to see things differently – including change –
has amazing results.*

Today's climate is laced with uncertainty and fear. We've all had to watch as the things that we've valued, and that have made us feel secure, disappear. Job security is a thing of the past, stability in relationships can't be taken for granted, and even our sense of personal safety has been shaken as we ask ourselves whether any place is safe to live and work. And, still there is hope. Our fear (often cleverly disguised as anger, depression, or loneliness, among other emotions) can be replaced with an awareness of our choices in life. The key to replacing fear lies in being able to shift our perceptions. Life's lessons are about getting up. If we focus on the spills and falls that are part of life's experience, we can miss the signposts that show us a better way to meet our challenges. This chapter is about the process of getting up.

Life's lessons are about getting up.

Over the centuries, much has been said and written about change. We all know that change is a never-ending process. Yet, despite the inevitability of change, we must keep in mind that growth is optional. We can't always change the events in our lives, but we can choose to change our perception of those events. We *can* choose to see life as a battleground where fear causes us to attack others and ourselves. We can choose blind acceptance of what *happens* to us. This choice leads to complacency and, ultimately to stagnation – another vision of the battleground. Or, we can choose to see life as a classroom, where we learn lessons. We can choose to experience life as a classroom – all we need is a little willingness.

As women, we are often working in professions or in volunteer roles that help others, while balancing family responsibilities, and wanting to make a difference in the lives of those around us. By helping others to see situations differently, we give them the encouragement that they need to make whatever changes they want in their lives. However, to be truly effective in helping others, we must begin with ourselves. It is not easy to 'practice what we preach', but, we can give only that which we have first given to ourselves. The shift in perception starts with us. It is important to keep in mind that perception is an interpretation, not a fact. This story recently reminded me of this:

> *I proudly gave a colleague my new business card. The card shows a picture of a glass half-filled with water. The words 'Real Choices' are written across it. My colleague stared at it and said, "Wow. You've made a bold statement." I enthusiastically agreed. She then said, "This is quite the statement." I again agreed, but more slowly, and commented that I was sure she knew the meaning of the glass of water. She assured me that she did. Then, leaning towards me, she whispered, "Are you a recovering alcoholic?"*
>
> *Shocked, I replied "No," and asked her where she had gotten that idea. She had thought that the words 'Real Choices' written across the glass of water meant 'drink water, not alcohol'. She had a friend who was a recovering alcoholic, and that friend had pictures of water all over her home to remind her to stay away from alcohol.*

My colleague's perception reflected her interpretation, but that perception was not a fact!

Creating Our Reality

The good news is that we can shift how we interpret events. Quantum physics teaches that *interpretation* is powerful enough to create the reality that we see. As demonstrated through the Heisenberg Uncertainty Principle, when scientists structured certain experiments in their labs to observe wave properties, they found wave properties. When they structured the same experiments to observe particles, they observed particles!

The good news is that we *can* shift our interpretation of events. In times of crises, I have often found the Chinese character symbol for crisis to be very comforting. The symbol has two parts: one means 'danger', and the other, 'opportunity'. Choosing opportunity is up to us. It is that simple ... but it is not always easy. However, knowing the choice opens us up to seeing possibilities and options.

Being able to shift perception is a powerful tool. One of my earliest realizations of this truth happened years ago in a class I was taking:

> *A woman sitting beside me was drawing arrows all over her paper. I equated arrows with guns and axes, and so, in a shocked tone, I asked why she was drawing them. She smiled at my strong reaction. She was just about to answer me when Ron, who was sitting on the opposite side, pointed out that she was drawing flowers. We argued back and forth, each of us wondering what was wrong with the other, until Ron finally took the book and turned it around. I suddenly realized that from where he was sitting, he saw flowers! It turned out that the woman was indeed drawing arrows, but not because she wanted 'to do someone in' (my perception). Rather, she felt that she needed direction, and arrows were her metaphor for that feeling. Shifting perception physically or mentally can make all the difference to your experience.*

No matter what the situation, if you are experiencing anxiety, fear, and uncertainty, always ask these questions: *"Is there another way to look at this? What am I learning?"* These questions instantly shift you into learning mode. However, there have been times I've reminded myself that the painful situation I'm experiencing is simply life learning, and still, my panic continues. That's not surprising, as I'm sure that we have all experienced challenges in learning. In such times, I've been inspired by the observation of one of my mentors, Holocaust survivor Viktor Frankl:

> *Everything can be taken away but one thing:*
> *the last of the human freedoms – to choose one's*
> *attitude in any given set of circumstances, to*
> *choose one's own way.*

But, Frankl's observation doesn't mean we should ignore danger, conflict, and challenges.

Choosing to See Things Differently

Once, a professor that I met at a conference in the States entertained me with his life stories. They seemed straight from a movie, yet the message about the choices we have were clear:

> *His marriage had gotten off to a rocky start when, a few weeks before it took place, his father announced that he was divorcing his mother to marry the fiancee's mother. By the time this professor was in his mid thirties, he and his wife each had a Ph.D., and had five children!*
>
> *The man's eyes were alive with laughter and happiness as he talked about his now grown children, who were professionally and financially very successful. When I told him that he seem to have had a happy life, he nodded in agreement and said that he had been fortunate. When I went on to say (with a touch of envy in my voice) that he'd been living the perfect life, he gently corrected me. He reminded me that he had never said his life was perfect.*
>
> *He told me that he had not mentioned the time his house burned down and there was no insurance to cover the loss. He also hadn't told me about the time his daughter (now a lawyer) had been in a car crash and then in a coma for months, and that she now walks with a cane. As he related these other events in his life, I expressed shock that he had described his life as being fortunate. He shrugged and replied that the negatives had also been part of his life; he just didn't dwell on them.*

Focusing on what isn't working in life can become an all-too-familiar pattern. We have only to listen to the conversations around us to know that many people feel quite comfortable in sharing tales of woe. Unfortunately, this behaviour keeps us stuck in the past. It is normal to want to stick to the familiar – to remain in our comfort zones. But then, we run the risk of stagnation. This is a good time to remember that we can choose to see things differently.

Desire for Change

Growth involves a desire for change and movement. All we need is a little willingness to see things differently. However, we will find that the path is not straightforward. Flashbacks, phantom pains, and backsliding are all part of the process. We can trust that we will find the necessary encouragement when the going seems rough. The encouragement may come in the form of a book, a workshop, a stranger on a train ... or countless other ways.

Always keep in mind what growth looks like. Picture a chart, with its mountains and valleys progressing from the bottom left-hand corner of your page to the top right-hand corner. Look carefully. Eventually, you'll see that today's valley was yesterday's mountaintop. It is important that we be there for ourselves, because when we are not, the valleys are extra painful, and the mountaintops are less joyful.

We often realize that a shift is necessary when pain or unhappiness arises. Some people seem to have a sixth sense: they can anticipate that change is needed, and then make the change. I know that such people exist ... but I'm not one of them! My professional life has involved writing and presenting on transitions and change, as I believe that we teach what we need to learn. I also believe that we don't have to hit rock bottom, with its agony, before realizing that our actions are not giving us the life we want. Knowing *inside* that there has to be a better way puts us on the road to change.

It's that simple. Yet, it's not an easy process. Have you ever gone through an experience in which your fears seemed groundless, and yet you felt paralyzed and unable to take action? Fears aren't about logic. We can easily stay stuck in the battleground, dealing with demons that we can't quite name, unable to make the shift to the classroom, where we can learn from our experience. By the way, simply acknowledging the experience puts us immediately into the classroom!

> *My son swims like a fish, and loves the water. That wasn't always the case: I remember taking him to swimming lessons, and watching him sit by the side of the pool while the other kids splashed through the class time. The teacher begged him to jump in. No way would he do it. His dad and I got into the water and promised to catch him. That made no difference. I tried bribing him with toys, food, television – anything that I thought would work. Nothing made the slightest difference. I kept up the lessons on and off for about 18 months. It was a family joke that we paid for Jason to sit by the pool and dangle his feet in the water.*

> *Then, one day, I looked up from a book I was reading. Jason was in the water. He was laughing and showing no sign of fear! Shocked, I asked him after the class what had made him get into the pool. He replied, "I wanted to." A little annoyed, I made some facetious comment to the effect that obviously all these months he hadn't wanted to. With the wisdom of a child, he ignored my remark. But, I think he was on to something.*

The desire to jump can overcome the fear that causes us to sit on the side of life. But, we may have to give that desire – that intention – time to strengthen. We (or well-meaning friends) cannot rush the process.

It was very affirming for me to read *Widowed*, by Dr. Joyce Brothers. She was brave enough to write about her fears surrounding the death of her husband of more than 30 years. She had been a wealthy woman in her own right, and she was now wealthier after his death. Yet, she was convinced that she would no longer be able to make it financially on her own. She was convinced that she would become destitute. Her evenings were spent going over and over her finances. Neither the reassurances of family members, nor her own knowledge that she was extremely wealthy, could help her feel secure. She had to arrive at that place in her own time.

I, too, was convinced that I would end up starving after my husband's death. The fact that I had always been able to support myself did nothing to banish my fears. Dr. Brothers showed me that fears have little to do with logic. I remember smiling as I read about her fears, which mirrored mine. To myself I said, "See, you're not odd. Others feel the same way!"

Time Out Exercise: Take a few minutes to think of a time when you accomplished something that you didn't think you could. What obstacles did you face? What helped you to succeed. Know that whatever helped you then can be transferred to other situations in the present.

The Four Stages of Change

Remember that every change involves a rite of passage: a period of discomfort, an initiation before adjustment. During that time, things may actually seem to get worse before they get better. Doubts appear, and FEAR ('false evidence appearing real'- original source of acronym unknown) seems to take on a life of its own. At these times, I like to remind myself of the sensations that

I feel in an airplane as it taxis down the runway. There's the excitement of knowing I'm finally on my way. Then, the plane slows down and stops ... before it speeds up and takes off.

In our own lives, those slowdown periods may last a minute, or several years. That's all right. They are part of our personal journeys. We need to take them at our own pace, and we cannot be rushed, nor rush through them. That idea is comforting to remember as you move through the four stages of change. The key is to be gentle with yourself as you go through your 'stuff' during the process of change. And, a sense of humour certainly makes for an easier trip. The four stages of change are:

Stage #1 - Awareness: Change begins with the awareness – sometimes like vague stirrings, sometimes like a whack on the head – that we need to do things differently. We need to create a space to allow more joy into our lives. A simple exercise to help get ego (the home of fear) out of the way is to write. Keep a journal without censoring thought, and without investing in a particular point of view. Later, go back and read what was written. You may be amazed at the clarity that you find in your own words!

Stage #2 - Intention: Next comes the intention, which is the desire for things to be different. At this point, you need clarity; vague feelings give vague results. Keep in mind that fear can rear its head during any of the four stages and this one is no exception.

For some time, I had realized that I wanted to finish my first book. I was certainly aware that my passions involved presenting and writing. I came face to face with my fears when I was doing workshops on a cruise ship:

> *The day after one of my workshops, a man and his wife approached me at breakfast. He told me how much they had enjoyed my presentation, and that I should write a book. I smiled, and told them that I was doing so. He then told me to give my business card to his wife. The realization struck me that they were in the publishing business, but I didn't have my card with me. Again, he asked me for a card. I hunted in my bag and couldn't find one. At that point, he gave a laugh and told me to enjoy my breakfast.*

> *I sat down, heart pounding, then I went to my cabin and got a card. When I returned, the couple had left the dining room. Why had I not asked their names, their room number? I could have made arrangements to get my card to them, but had not. I could have written down my contact information, but had not.*

At that point, I had to admit that my fear of success was so strong that I was sabotaging myself – and not for the first time! I had a choice: either stop talking about writing a book, or write the book! I realized that I couldn't do it on my own. I had become skilled at getting in my own way. One of the first things I did when I returned home was to hire a coach. I explained what my intentions were, and I asked him to help me stay focused. One of my first assignments was to join the Canadian Association of Professional Speakers (CAPS). That gave me a supportive environment in which to stay on task. Nine months later, I gave birth to my book, *That Perception Thing!*

Having the intention – the desire – means supporting it. That means creating the environment in which it can happen. Negativity or vagueness about intentions will not provide the climate for you to soar. Years ago, I read somewhere that if you want to fly like an eagle, you can't scratch with the turkeys!

Stage #3 – Go About Your Business: The next step is to go about your business. Do the things that you need to do to support your intention, but also get busy with the other areas of your life. Although this is the time to take action, I agree with the saying that 'a watched pot never boils'. That misguided vigilance is right up there with the "are we there yet" question that can often take the fun out of travelling.

At this stage, practise non-attachment to the outcome. Again, fear can appear as we agonize about doing the 'right' thing, and second-guess ourselves. Reaching out for the next step inevitably means leaving something behind. This stage is challenging. You're preparing the space for what is to come, but you're also grieving what has to go. And, you don't know what is coming your way, or what additional changes it will bring. We must remember to go about our business, to have fun, and not to insist on the outcome happening in a certain way.

Stage #4 – Manifestation: The final stage is manifestation — the outcome. It often will not look like or be what we thought or expected. It comes with its own unique set of changes and fears. Let's face it: getting what we want can be terrifying. A friend recently met the person she described as 'the love I've been waiting for'. Their happiness was obvious to all, and that was when she started noticing the little annoying things about him that eventually caused her to leave.

It is important to set your intentions at the highest level: *for the good of all.* It does affect your outcome. I came across a cartoon that showed a couple celebrating the husband's 60th birthday. He looks at his wife, who looks 60 years old, and then he makes a wish as he blows out his candles. He wishes he were married to a woman 25 years younger than he. As the smoke from all the candles clears, we see him with a shocked look on his face. He gets his wish; he is now 85 years old!

Tools to Move Through Change

Many tools and techniques help us to move through the process of change. The following section will provide you with some of these 'tools' that will assist you with thriving with changes in your life:

Self-Care: The first thing we need to do is the necessary self-care that communicates to us that we matter, that we are worthwhile. It is so easy in relationships or in the workplace to put the needs of others first. That soon means that we no longer have anything to give. Yet, we keep on giving. Before we know it, we're on the back burner of our own lives, and running on empty. We then become stressed out – pulled in too many directions.

When we lose touch with self, we become needy. Neediness is not attractive. Being there for self means that when we reach out to others, we do so from a position of strength, as opposed to one of desperation. This applies in all areas of life. Sad to say, those who convey desperation in a job search will often not be hired. They are so focused on their needs that they are unable to communicate what they can offer to the organization. I also have yet to hear anyone say, *"I've met the most clinging, needy, insecure person ... I think I'm in love!"*

The brilliant writer, Merle Shain, sums it up best:

> *Until you divest yourself of the notion that you*
> *are a collection of needs, an empty vessel that*
> *someone else must fill up, there will be no safe*
> *place to harbor yourself, no safe shore to reach.*
> *As long as you think mostly of getting, you will*
> *have nothing real to give.*

Laughter: Is there laughter in your life? We tend to take ourselves too seriously. Laughter offers a lightness of heart that can give us the willingness to allow awareness to emerge. Through it, we can gain insights to the barriers our fears have created. Laughter has the power to create the shifts necessary for us to see options and possibilities. It is a vehicle that can help us to find release from the build-up of 'stuff' in our lives. Laughter creates the flow of energy that can downgrade the storm of a crisis to a mere drizzle, thus freeing us to take action.

Self-Talk: It is important that we monitor our self-talk. We think approximately 50,000 thoughts per day. About half of those thoughts are about ourselves, and 80% of those thoughts are negative. Such thinking can make change more difficult and painful than it need be. Years ago, I learned a technique that I've taught to others and have continued to use myself. It's taken from the Rational Emotive approach to therapy by Albert Ellis, and is an excellent way to look at what we're creating with our thoughts. The ABC exercise has three points, and can be done in your head or on paper.

A	The Activating Event
B	Beliefs about the Event
C	Emotional Consequences

For example, if you apply for a new job and do not get it (A), you may feel angry or depressed (C). You interpret your feelings (C) as being caused by not getting the job (A). However, that skips over your *interpretation* about not getting the job (B). If you believe you weren't hired because either you made a mess of the interview, or you were not smart enough, or the selection committee was biased, then that interpretation (B) – and not the event itself – leads to the emotional response. Understanding this process is a powerful way to shift perception. We shift from looking at who did what, or who said what, to challenging our interpretation. And, such a challenge can make all the difference!

Forgiveness: In closing, I want to acknowledge the role forgiveness plays in helping us to let go of our critical beliefs, and to move on. It is the choice to release grievances, to not tie our energies up in making anyone wrong. Much has been written about the need to forgive others and ourselves. Intellectually, we may acknowledge the importance of forgiveness, but emotionally, we may feel trapped, mired in the pain of who did what to whom. As we rehash the past, a feeling arises of being unable (or unwilling) to break this pattern that brings no joy. It takes a tremendous amount of negative energy to keep the past alive in our present. Forgiveness is an ongoing lesson, and a tool that we can use to help us move through further lessons.

*If our choice is to have more joy in our
lives, we give a gift to ourselves. The choice
is always ours!*

Biography for Dawn Brown

Business Name: Perception Shift
Address: 73 Atholldoune Street,
                     Aylmer, Quebec, J9J 1H9
Telephone: (819) 770-3739
Email: dcosmob@hotmail.com
Web Address: www.perceptionshift.com

Canadian Association of Professional Speakers Chapter:
Ottawa, Associate Member

About Dawn:

Dawn Brown, M. Ed. (counselling) has extensive experience as a teacher, psychotherapist, and trainer specializing in career and life transitions. Her presentations are designed to inspire listeners and participants to reach higher levels of achievement in all areas of life. Her keynote and seminar topics include: *'Discovering Your Emotional Intelligence'*, *'Managing Change'*, *'Emotional Healing'*, *'Self Care Starts with You'*, and *'Choosing Opportunity'*.

Dawn's presentations are described as inspiring, educational, genuine, entertaining and *'just what I needed to hear'*. Her insights are the results of years of experience in the health, educational, and counselling professions, and are shared with audiences large and small because *'I teach what I need to learn'*. Her message is simple yet effective: we can't always change the events in our lives but we can choose to change our perceptions of them!

In addition to being a member of CAPS, Dawn is also a member of the Canadian Counselling Association, and the International Federation of Facilitators. She is currently the Director of Student Life Services at Carleton University.

Dawn's Publications:

- That Perception Thing! (Creative Bound Inc, 2002)
- 'On the Couch', in the ezine, Energy Medicine Online.

Out of Frantic ...
Into Focus

By: Pauline Duncan-Thrasher
Ignite A Spark Speaking

Learning how to be focused when dealing with life's challenges.

Have you ever felt like a cat chasing its tail, or a gerbil running inside a little plastic ball, and getting nowhere? When money worries threaten to overpower you, or a disastrous relationship leaves you feeling threadbare, or work and home responsibilities keeping you running without making progress: stop! Take a deep breath, and remember that there are strategies that will help.

Regardless of age or income, we all feel frantic sometimes. Dealing with everyday challenges might include any, or all, of the following: Will I ever find a beloved, special person? How will I cope with losing a loved one? Will I be able to stay healthy, and deal calmly with aging? How will I ever learn to conquer the deadly paper dragon? Can I discover how to cram 30 hours of living into a 24-hour day? How can I remain calm while I manoeuver the transitions of life? How can I reach, and maintain, my cherished independence? How can I find, keep, and ultimately, retire, from a satisfying career?

> *Frantic souls miss the possibilities. Calm ones see many options.*

To make the necessary transitions from frantic to focused behaviour, we need to change our habits. Instead of feeling helpless, we can develop the self-confidence that comes from 'taking charge' of our lives.

> *"If you always do what you've always done, you'll always get what you've always got!"*
> - *Peter Urs Bender, writer and speaker*

Reading the 18 strategies in this chapter will assist you to meet the challenges of everyday life, and turn tragedies into triumphs. Picture yourself responding with the focused behaviour that will give you greater success, inner serenity, and happiness. Imagine feeling calm, strong, and happy with your life — challenges and all!

A Personal Awakening

We all have a story to tell. Mine happened in the balmy Caribbean waters of Honduras, more than 20 years ago.

My travelling companion and diving buddy had decided to sleep in on the cloudy, last day of our adventure in a remote divers' paradise. Because I was determined to dive one last time before returning home — and contrary to all safe diving practices — I dove without a buddy. Delighting in the wonders of colorful underwater life, I was oblivious to the diminishing contents of my oxygen tank. I surfaced once to check on the boat (directly above me) and, although my oxygen was nearly gone, went back down for one final, quick look. As I surfaced, my snorkel accidentally fell out of my suit. I let it go, and swam to the top. There was nothing but waves under a graying sky. I twisted anxiously in the choppy water, searching for the dive boat. Way in the distance, I could see a small dot.

That's when my frantic feelings began to churn! My mind quickly thought of the horror of drowning, and my body being lost at sea, and the boat owner going to tell my friend that my body had just disappeared. Although assistive tools were close, I felt too panicked to use them. Some misguided notion of frugality caused me to keep my diving weights anchored around my waist. A quick attempt to blow up my Buoyancy Compensator (B.C.) in the wavy waters failed, so I began to swim. You can imagine my bargaining talk with God. "I'm too happy to die yet. If you let me survive, I'll …". When fatigue robbed my arms of momentum, or I'd swallowed too many mouthfuls of water, I floated face down. I prayed a lot, and swam as much as one can with waist weights and a tank on the back. Friends later asked why I hadn't just unstrapped the empty tank, and floated on it.

The terror of drowning suppressed all logic, but staying calm made the difference between life and death. About the time that I saw the boat after surfacing, those on board realized that I was not with them. As they prepared to move in my direction, their motor gave out. In retrospect, they must have been feeling almost as frantic, on that boat, as I was in the water. When we finally caught up to each other, the Captain called out, "Do you want to just hold on for awhile, or do you want to climb up?" Clinging to the gloved hand of the boat owner replaced my panic with comfort.

I could have drowned in the Caribbean, through forgetting to implement safety procedures that I had practiced so many times before, in diving classes. How often do we overlook tools that enable us to help ourselves? How many times do we ignore safety precautions designed to keep us healthy? How often do we flounder, too proud to ask someone for advice or assistance?

I've never been much of a drinker, but that day I got drunk for the first — and last— time in my life. It only took a few, long swallows of the bottle of island rum that was passed around on the boat. I went back to our small room, and tearfully told my friend that I had nearly drowned. We returned to the boat to enjoy a popcorn party in celebration of my survival.

There's nothing like a near-death experience to act as a catalyst for an individual's true appreciation of life. I knew that nearly drowning was the result of my own self-centered gratification and carelessness. But, I also realized the benefits of calling on inner strength and God. Between swimming and praying, my eyes never left the 'rescue ship'. Talk about focus! In those potentially panic-filled moments, my single-minded goal to reach that safe haven kept terror from drowning me.

"You are the product of what you choose for yourself in every life situation. By being ever alert for turning adversity around, and by fearlessly implementing risk-taking alternatives, you'll soon be gratified by the way your life can take a turn for the better."
*   - Dr. Wayne Dyer, author and speaker*

Life Strategies

The following 18 points will assist your move from 'frantic to focused' in your own life.

1. Learn to Accept and to Change: Although the following is often referred to as the 'AA Prayer', it has a wisdom so simple, and straightforward, that it can apply to anyone, of any age, with any problem.

The Serenity Prayer

God grant me the serenity to accept the things
I cannot change,
Courage to change the things I can,
And wisdom to know the difference.

The secret to tranquility is to gain a perspective of our priorities, and to discover what we can change, and what we need to just accept. The next time a problem screams into your face, apply the Serenity Prayer, and make a choice – change the situation, or accept it. At a time in life when my world seemed to be capsizing, Wayne Dyer's book, *Your Erroneous Zones,* appeared. Years later, when that wonderful author appeared at a conference, I was able to tell him in person how much his book had helped me to change my life responses. It is a book worth reading for anyone who appreciates the message of the Serenity Prayer.

2. Enjoy the excitement of determining and reaching goals: Can you recapture the excitement of dreams that you had as a child? Remember how excited you felt when you finally were able to get the adult to say *'maybe',* to your incessant requests to go for a sleepover, or a movie, or a trip to the beach? Children seem to have the ability to relentlessly pursue their desires. Many will not take *'No'* for an answer.

As adults, we sometimes become easily side-tracked from our life's dreams. At an open audition for a choice training position, I once used a pair of greasy binoculars to represent the shadowy glimpses that distort our view, in contrast to the vivid sight we gain when looking through clear glass.

> Knowing what we want is like looking through clean binoculars. Keeping a clear-sighted, positive vision gives us a head start on goal achievement.

As adults, we have the potential to turn our dreams into reality. What if you took time to calmly put on paper what you most want from life, then created a clear set of steps to achieve that dream? Use the techniques described by Shakti Gawain in the best seller *Creative Visualization*. You, too, can become the enthusiastic person who pursues and achieves dreams through clear vision.

3. Build and maintain a positive self-esteem through positive self-talk: Make a list of your most successful achievements. Read your list aloud every day. Know that those strengths will carry you through all challenges. If you cannot think of any strengths, ask a friend or your mentor for suggestions. When you are having a horrible day, remember your successes, and take time to realize the lessons that you are learning.

4. Choose an inspiring mascot: One writer told about keeping a thistle on his desk, because of the following belief: If you reach out and grab it quickly, it won't hurt. If you are frightened, and touch it too timidly, it will smart. One of my favorite symbols is the duck. Watch the constantly moving webbed feet of a duck. They appear quiet on the surface, yet are busy underwater. Small irritations that cause some of us to rant and rave just float over the heads of calm people — like water over a duck's back.

5. Develop your spiritual health through daily meditation and prayer: Prayer life can be a steadfast, calming anchor. With maturity and personal losses, often comes a richer, more heartfelt spirituality. Many of us find harmony and peace within a church community. You've probably discovered that, for many, spiritual strength comes from within. Meditation and prayer are proven stress relievers. Many people also enjoy the soothing relief that comes from time spent away from the rushing, noisy lifestyle of the city, in quiet parks or the country.

> *Go placidly amidst the noise and haste*
> *And know what peace there may be in silence.*
>
> *Desiderata*

6. Develop a working relationship with a reliable, knowledgeable mentor: We can learn so much from someone who has gone through the wringer, and managed to come out intact. Nourishing positive relationships allows us breathing time to learn how to better manage our lives. Receiving and giving positive, constructive tips builds a win-win relationship. And, sometimes, the teacher learns as much as the student. Don't be afraid to ask someone you admire to be your mentor. Establish a mutually satisfactory schedule that will be flexible enough to accommodate both of your needs. Then, enjoy the mutual *journey of growth.*

7. Nurture your physical well-being by making daily smart choices: Healthy eating, plenty of rest, and making time to exercise are areas that we can control. These good habits can be developed, and will sustain us through the tough times.

> *Expanding your lunch break from 15 to 30*
> *minutes will not only energize you, but also*
> *slash your stress levels by 50 percent or more.*
>
> *- Ellen Dunn, Ph.D.*

It is too difficult to handle the challenges of a busy work schedule with less than a full night's sleep. We have all experienced the fatigue that comes from poor eating, and hours sitting in front of a computer. If we spent one tenth of the time on maintaining a healthy body that many spend on a car, we would all be in great shape!

Practicing deep breathing techniques is a stress reliever. Consciously breathing from the diaphragm only takes a few minutes, but the results are amazing. Try doing this when you feel worn out or ready to scream with exasperation. You will be amazed at the soothing effect of deep breathing on your mind and body.

8. Find an interesting job. Do you choose to be stressed, or exhilarated for eight or more hours a day? Isn't our work a key to our happiness? There may be days for you when you think, "Please — no more challenges!" But, aren't the challenges making your life interesting?

"Boredom is nearly twice as stressful as activity. Finding a job with a few more ups or downs could slash your stress levels by a whopping 200%."

- Murray Carpenter, Ph.D.

9. Develop Assertiveness Skills: By knowing how to say 'yes' or 'no' (or as my esteemed friend Doug says *"Let me get back to you on that"*), we establish control in our lives. A person in control is a person who is not only focused, but free of the many stressors that come from trying to please everyone but ourselves. Assertiveness is about taking charge of our lives. It is the secret to success, health, and happiness. Voicing our opinions, speaking up for our rights, and following our own standards develops not only self-respect, but the earned respect of everyone we meet. Assertiveness is the mark of maturity and good health of mind and spirit.

10. Take Time to Laugh: My mother often voiced this old saying, *"Laugh and the world laughs with you. Cry and you cry alone"*. Our world needs more 'laughers'. There are three people in my life who embody this. Tanys and Bonnie are sisters, whom I've known for a while, and Sue came into my life recently. All three have been the best laughers, and have been challenged the most physically. Their laughter seems to have pulled them through the toughest times when most of us would have just given up, kicked our wheelchairs to pieces, and lay down to die.

Good, deep belly laughs have been proven to release a stress-relieving chemical that does make us feel better. The benefits of laughter go way more than skin deep. If you take life very seriously, try to hang around with those who like to laugh. Some of that laughter may rub off.

11. If you need professional help, get it: Many of us have experienced times when we have felt frantic, depressed, strained, drained, and hopeless. That terrible, paralyzing panic may develop into inertia that makes us believe it is easier and safer to do nothing, so we stop struggling. We keep quiet, even when we yearn to scream. We choke back tears, and act as though we do not care. Most of us would not consider walking around with a broken leg. Why do we hesitate to ask for help when we are no longer able to deal with stress?

The greatest shame in waiting to get help is that we waste precious years suffering. Our world is filled with people who have become stronger, once they recognized their need, and found help. Breaking out of any self-imposed shell is never an easy task. Habitual hermits may require significant help to make the final break. The assistance is always available, just as my buoyancy compensator and floatable oxygen tank were. But, I needed to reach out to get help. So may you. Do it now.

12. *Live life one day at a time:* How many times have you lost sleep over upcoming events, or agonized over past events? Most of us spend far too much time worrying over what we did or didn't do yesterday, or fussing about what will happen next month, or next year. A smart person once compared time to money.

> *Yesterday is a cancelled cheque. Tomorrow is a promissory note.*
> *Today is the only cash you have. Spend it while you can.*
> *- Original source unknown*

13. *Clear out the clutter:* If you're a pack rat like me, this will be a challenge. Start with one room. It is amazing what a sense of calm uncluttering can create. So much stress and wasted time for me came from searching for lost papers, keys, and books. My husband put up a key rack, just inside our kitchen. That small act, and a few reminders to yours truly to put keys where they belonged, relieved my many moments of frantic searching for the house key, the school key, the car key. As you clear the paper clutter, other areas seem easier to manage. Try it. You'll like it.

14. *Break projects into workable steps:* Who among us has not put off a big task, and suffered hours of stress? Procrastination can be as deadly as the plague. Whether it is cleaning out the closet, completing a term paper, hiring a new staff member, or applying for a new position, we delay until we need to race, and cut corners. One first step, however small, immediately relieves that frantic feeling. By working for small amounts of time, we increase our productivity, and feel once more in control. The best antidote for stress is POSITIVE ACTION!

15. *Practice saying 'Oops' when you make a mistake:* We all make mistakes, and aiming for perfection only makes everyone anxious. Get on with it! The quantity of what you can accomplish will immediately improve, and quality is not far behind. We need to be more forgiving with ourselves. In the words of that wonderful television series, 'Life Goes On!'

16. Get the knots out of the hose: We all need connections based on healthy esteem. Connections based on insecurity, however, can be as lethal as poison. These can include: parent-child relationships that teeter on over-dependency, working relationships that tear away self-esteem, sibling relationships filled with jealousy, peer relationships built on dominance and submission, or spousal relationships that lack communication. By staying in these relationships, we are ingesting daily doses of deadly poison. We need to find a way out.

I'm a fairly new gardener. If you're like me, there are times when you get the hose to the flower, squeeze the trigger, and the water just doesn't flow. You find yourself retracing your steps to discover that there is a knot in the hose. Once you untangle the knot the water starts to flow freely. Knots in our lives that block the flow of energy can come from unhealthy relationships, ungrieved deaths of loved ones, or our inability to get what we want. We need to take the time to untangle the knots in our lives. We need to tap back into the power that is within.

You may have had a lot of 'knots' in your life, or only struggled with one or two. A famous speaker (whose name I unfortunately cannot recall) tells this story:

> *A hound dog was sitting on the front porch, whining and howling. When someone asked what ailed the dog, the answer was quick: "Oh, he's sitting on a nail". "Why doesn't he get off the nail?" "Well, I guess it doesn't hurt enough."*
> *- Original source unknown*

How many of us endure unpleasant, life draining situations far longer than necessary because the familiar is easier to withstand? Sometimes, we act only when the status quo becomes unbearable.

> **When we finally relinquish the mantle of hurt, and start to embrace the jacket of life, we realize that time does indeed soften even the most brutal hurt.**

17. Tap into the source of power: Sometimes, special friendships energize us in a way that no doctor's medicine ever can. Replenishing your energies with spiritual and physical sustenance must be a priority if you are to stand on your own feet, as a healthy individual. For, it is only as a healthy person, that you can begin to reach out to others with the compassion and love that enrich both giver and receiver.

> *Recently, my Aunt Rita died. She was 82. My mother and my father's family had been estranged for most of my life. A short time after my mother died, I reacquainted my grown self with my father's sister – my aunt Rita. She had never married, and had combined several careers as social worker, missionary nun, and school bus driver. She had lived independently as a career woman, at home with her elderly mother and, for the last 32 years, alone, yet she never seemed lonely. She engaged in numerous correspondences with people all over the world, tracing family genealogies. She was known to most of the 2,300 people in her small hometown. She combined a quiet, sometimes stubborn independence with a ready sense of humour, an inquisitive mind, and a simple generosity of spirit that earned her many friends of all ages. Our daylong visits involved chatting, going for lunch, sightseeing, and just enjoying each other's company. Aunt Rita accepted me into her life. Our mutual admiration was a simple pleasure for both of us as we grew to be kindred spirits. I had lived alone for 20 years, and related well with her independent spirit. She seemed a little apprehensive of my late-in-life marriage, but soon grew to accept and like my husband. Aunt Rita had saved all of the pictures that appeared in the newspaper of me, and carefully dated them. She had even written names of my relatives on a scrap of paper. She did not need to make a fuss when I came to visit, because we felt at home together. Despite surgery, and the threat of chemotherapy, my aunt continued to plan bus trips and outings with friends until the day she died.*

Non-demanding relationships are both rare and priceless. If you have a relative or a friend like my Aunt Rita, seize as many opportunities as possible to share time with that person. An accepting relationship is good for the soul. Search out your neglected relatives, or volunteer to befriend someone who needs a visit. Nursing homes are filled with people who rarely receive visits. In discovering your own ability to accept others as they are, you will become a stronger, happier person.

18. Believe in your positive power. Ignite your own sparks of energy:

Looks Good to Me!

When I look in the mirror, who do I see?
Who is the person who stares back at me?
Do I only see scars, lines, crooked nose?
Can I cherish the beauty of this flawed, unique rose?

Do I fuss about hair that seems out of place —
Or accept, with a grin, this irreplaceable face?
Do I worry about age, and time that won't stop —
Or thank the good Lord that still feel tiptop?
And, if perchance, I am sick for a while —
Can I wisely remember my treasures and smile?

To Feel, Hear, Speak, Love
And yes, to say 'NO' to a shove.
For these, I thank my good Lord up above.
My flaws, my strengths, the everyday 'Joe' —
The whole package is me- I'm just starting to know.

The friends, family, strangers, and judges I meet,
Have never travelled inside my two feet.
I must love and support the child hidden inside.
Finally, lose that desperate desire to hide.
Of life's struggles, I can say, I'm not perfect, and yet,
There are wonderful treasures I'm still able to get.

Who is really my very best friend?
The friend in the mirror who can love, lose, still bend.
When I look in the mirror, who do I see?
Whoever she is – she looks GOOD to me!

- Pauline Duncan-Thrasher

Biography for Pauline Duncan-Thrasher

Business Name: Ignite A Spark!
Address: 88 Beechbank Crescent
London, Ontario N6E 2P3
Telephone: (519) 681-3774
Email: dthrasher@odyssey.on.ca

Canadian Association of Professional Speakers Chapter:
Southwestern Ontario, Associate Member

About Pauline:
Positive Pauline enables participants to recognize their power within. Keynotes and workshops include: *'Ignite the Spark!'* *'Out of Frantic...Into Focus'*, *'Victim to Victor'* and *'Personal Possibilities'*. Pauline has spoken on Ottawa's Parliament Hill, and at the Canada Club in Toronto, and hosted her own television series.

She is an educator, winning speaker, and evaluator and past district governor for Toastmaster's International. Clients have included the Canadian Mental Health Association, GM Diesel, Canada Trust, Fanshawe College, and the University of Western Ontario.

Come To The Edge...

By: Carole Kent
Edge-Rider International

"Great spirits have always encountered violent opposition from mediocre minds."
-Albert Einstein

He stared at me every time I entered my workroom. It was easy for him – dominating one whole wall – looking out from two, huge, gold-trimmed prints. This time, I decided to stare back at Albert Einstein. I sat, transfixed, and let my mind free fall to…

- being 'a great spirit', having the courage to open my mind, and embrace possibilities never considered before
- being brave enough to make resourceful choices, even under the most constricting circumstances, and
- making a profound difference in the world.

"Albert", I said aloud, as though I knew him personally, *"What inspired you anyway? How did you stay centred in the midst of chaos and change?"* My own inner voice responded quickly, "I know! You kept expanding your growth edges, to form ever-widening circles of influence. You could go over the edge of limitation, and become the dream. You were an edge-rider!"

'EDGE-RIDER!!!' My company name was born. Along with it came a flood of ideas, memories, and questions about my own life:

- Memories of pivotal experiences and challenges flashed to mind.
- Would I let go of suffering, and choose vital health for a lifetime?
- Would I let go of popular opinion about the inevitability of disease?
- Would I speak from my own integrity, intuition, and learning?
- Would I be open to receive all the gifts these positive choices would bring?

I said yes.
I became an Edge-Rider.
May I inspire you!

1. What Is An Edge-Rider?

An Edge-Rider is a modern-day pioneer who is vision-driven and solution-oriented. This person will not only take the road less travelled, but will pave the way for others to follow. Malcolm Gladwell, in his book called, *The Tipping Point*, provides an incentive to be an Edge-Rider. His profoundly hopeful message is *"that one imaginative person applying a well-placed lever, can move the world."*

Edge-Riders want to make a difference in this world.

2. Edge-Riders Have A Dream

"I Have A Dream…"
- Martin Luther King

Those are four powerful words. They still resonate around the world, and people can picture the dream and the man – Martin Luther King. He is a touchstone for our world vision of freedom, peace, and opportunity.

When we can define our dream clearly, we have a compelling reason to move forward with it every single day. When we can state the dream clearly in a sentence or two, we can seriously act upon it. A sentence or two! A whole dream in a sentence or two. Such economy of thought seemed impossible for me until a little guide called 'synchronicity' came to help me out.

The Dream Of Women Worldwide

My task was to prepare a speech for a women's networking group. Trying to emphasize the importance of wellness to business success, I developed this snappy title, 'It's Healthy to be Successful'. Just as I was about to reference a favourite book by Dan Sullivan, I got sidetracked by the daily newspaper (The Hamilton Spectator, August 17, 2000). It fell open at the business section, and this information glared up at me. In a poll of 30,000 women in 33 countries worldwide, three major concerns surfaced repeatedly:

- women want financial independence (preferably by starting their own businesses)
- women want easier access to high quality health care, and
- women also want more balance in their lives, and more leisure time.

"If we don't take care of ourselves first, we can't take care of others." This was the collective cry of the women interviewed.

Wow! I pulled out the book that was tucked under my arm, and flipped to the page I had book marked. Dan Sullivan had cited the same points as the women. Health, Money, and Time were essential, and Health is foundational for everything. It was time to get my dream down on paper!

My Dream

By my words and actions, may I inspire you to reach a level of health and prosperity beyond your wildest imaginings. May your choices give you the freedom to enrich others, and strengthen the health of the planet.

There is a saying, *"When you state it, you create it."* (original source unknown). Writing your dream down and seeing it in print is powerful. In two sentences, try to write your dream:

_____

_____

_____

_____

_____

Edge-Riders dream and they make their dreams come true – but not alone. There's a saying accredited to the Beatles: *'I'll get by with a little help from my friends.'* A poster, given to me by a friend, and hanging from my filing cabinet, assures me of that. By offering their wisdom and expertise, friends become the guiding lights along the way. By sounding a cautionary note when we need it, friends become the warning lights that help redirect our focus. By celebrating with us in joy, friends become the neon lights that shout out our achievements.

Cultivated, loving friendship is a 'gift that keeps on giving'.

3. Edge-Riders Have Good Habits.

> *"We first make our habits, and then our habits make us."*
> *-John Dryden*

If a habit is an automatic response, why not have it working in our favour? The quality of our life depends on the quality of the questions we ask. Consider these:

- Do I value my personal health?
- Do I believe I can have good health for a lifetime?
- What does good health look like?
- Am I ready to change habits and beliefs that may undermine my health?

You might also add:
- Will I need a crisis to be my change agent?

A pivotal experience was my wake-up call.

At The Edge

My personal health plan was set in motion many years ago and was born out of challenge and frustration.

> *At age forty-nine my mother was diagnosed with ALS, Amyotropic Lateral Sclerosis (better known as Lou Gehrig's Disease). With the diagnosis, she was given a pamphlet about her disease which we started reading together at the hospital. It detailed the horror to come, step-by-step, and even predicted her probable death in three to four years. I was horrified. My mother must have been terrified.*
>
> *Dad, Mom and I immediately went into denial. We stayed there for the duration of her illness. We seemed to be trapped in a horror story with fear as a constant companion, and loss as the driving force. We got confirmation everyday that we were powerless, and we would have to accept the inevitable. Doctors told us so. Everybody who ever knew anybody with a serious illness told us so. Who were we to challenge these strong voices?*

So, we played our parts admirably. Mom used her sense of humour to ease our awkwardness, as her vibrancy changed to a shuffle, and her limbs finally refused to move. Dad worked for himself as a carpenter/contractor, and could only accept small jobs at this time of escalating costs; he chose to help Mom as often as he could. Still, she was alone for hours at a time, always fearing a fall. I was teaching in a city four hours away by car. Predictably and lovingly, I came every weekend and holiday, usually with my small son in tow, who provided the only loving relief we had. We persevered. We all tried to be cheerful when we really wanted to cry because of sheer exhaustion.

It was September. School had barely started when I was called to my mother's side for the last time. One journey was ending, but another was about to begin. The doctor spoke to me for the final time. He reminded me of our family history of MS and ALS, and other nerve diseases. He thought I should stay informed, and reminded me that males were more at risk, and, "You have a son".

That was it! My *intention* became crystal clear:

- Genetics will not trap me. The suffering will stop.
- Wellness – not illness – will be my focus
- Vibrant good health will be my journey.
- I will share my knowledge with everyone.

My mother had given me a tremendous gift – the determined resolve to take responsibility for my own health. Now, it was up to me to give the gift to the world. It was time to be an Edge-Rider.

A strong intention starts a cascade of events that keeps the dream alive.

At first, people started showing up in my life to invite me to learn about emotional and spiritual matters. From 'A Course in Miracles', to 'One Minute Wisdom', from 'Mind-mapping' to 'A Vision Quest', from meditations to affirmations, my 'teachers' showed me the value of starting from 'the inside out'. It would prove invaluable when a personal health crisis came to test my resolve.

My kidneys – after years of stress, no rest, and abuse from repeat prescriptions of antibiotics – wanted to shut down completely. That got my attention – painfully. How could my body protect itself now? The answer came as I was pouring fresh water into the dog's dish, and saw him lapping it up with gusto. With drugs we had only been treating the symptoms – the infections and the pain – and not looking at the cause, dehydration. (No doctor had ever asked me if I drank water.) To allow the cells to regenerate and my kidney to heal itself, water was going to be my best 'medicine', and a habit I would keep for good.

Amazingly, it was the water bottle in my hand that led me to the people who would teach me a lot more about the wonders of water and the wonders of food. Many good habits would follow.

4. Edge-Riders Are Team Players

> **Edge-Riders don't just expand their own growth edges. Their dreams intersect with the dreams of others, and the circle of life becomes more encompassing.**

Because we are committed to wellness as the foundation of life, my global team and my local team have much in common.

My Global Team

At the water's edge overlooking Klamath Lake, Oregon, I stood absolutely still. Extending my arms outward, as if reaching for my best friend, I embraced the magnificence of this ecological paradise. Whispering a silent prayer, I gave thanks for the ancient wild food it offered, an organic sunshine food that regenerated my body and spirit. On a lodgepole pine, perched like a 'Great Spirit', a Bald Eagle stared at me.

I felt as if I had stepped into the *'Sacred Circle'* painted by Bev Doolittle, the one that centres the wall above my computer station. There, in my workroom, *'Eagle'* stares at me every day. The painting reminds me of the uniqueness of our individual dreams, brought together to create a larger vision. Nine separate paintings come together to form a collective masterpiece when the significant element of each frame connects to form a 'Sacred Circle'.

I thought of the masterpiece that was being created here in Klamath Falls as significant individuals gathered from different parts of the world to share a collective dream – *'May all be fed. May all be healed. May all be loved.'*

This statement was authored by John Robbins. An eloquent spokesperson who gets standing ovations, even at the United Nations, his powerful message is full of hope. *"It is possible to make a difference in the environment, world hunger, and in your own personal health, by making a change in your eating habits."*

This man has truly inspired me. Some of the things I have learned from John Robbins are: Animals currently raised for food are often exposed to profoundly inhumane and unhealthy conditions that impact our physical, emotional, and economic health.

I have learned to challenge the beliefs on which health care is based, to move from disease care to health care, to question current methods of treating women and children, and to challenge the practice of over-medication and unnecessary suffering. I have learned to take responsibility for my own health. Prevention, especially through nutrition, is key. It can also be fun. Through the years, I have learned about the energetics of food, the power of raw foods, the benefits of macrobiotic cooking, the connections between food and behaviour, and the ways our animal friends can be better nourished. It has been a joyous journey.

My Local Team

The barn cats sit like little statues, set at peculiar angles, framing the pond, partly hidden by flowers. It's early Saturday morning, and *The Organic Farm* market will soon be open. As I push the barn door to enter, sunlight follows, and the young owner greets me with her usual warm smile, and a hug. I have been volunteering here for two years now, and love it. As the smell of roasted granola and oatmeal muffins fills the air, I set up my blender. Today, I will make 'smoothies' for people to sample. Combining the farm's organic fruit, ground flaxseeds, almond butter, and a dash of superfood, we have a heart-healthy drink to power us through the day. There are always 'demos', and tours of the barn to explain about the hundreds of organic, and natural items for sale. There are workshops about raw food and sprouting, wheat-free cooking, and healthy school lunches, to name a few.

In this toxic world, it is joyful to know we are offering people safe, healthy, delicious food that won't contaminate our bodies, our minds, or our environment. By our food choices, we can support local organic farmers who are not subsidized by the government or big business. By our food choices, we keep ourselves well, protect our precious topsoil from chemical pollution, and keep honeybees, butterflies, and birds from dying.

5. Edge-Riders Take Action

Over the years, my circles of connection keep growing and overlapping. Active Edge-Riders inform my life and my dream. Relationships deepen as we support each other's journey to wellness and prosperity. Together we have more to offer.

Action Team 1

Seated at friendly round tables, with the sun streaming across the harbour and in through the windows to greet us, we begin our monthly meeting. Tuesday morning at the yacht club, we gather as the *Health Professionals Network*. We are small business owners who have chosen to make our living by being of service to others. Today we each have three minutes for an infomercial – to exchange information, knowledge and professional resources. The two women co-founders know there are many ways to wellness – to attain it and keep it. As we applaud each other's unique offerings of health care, the affection for one another is obvious, and the joy genuine. We share expertise as nutritionists, fitness coaches, doctors of naturopathy, chiropractors, reflexologists, family counsellors, nurses in private practice, energy workers, acupuncturists, reiki masters and live blood microscopists…to name a few. We give workshops together, we hike together, we attend each other's special events, and we purchase each other's products and services. We keep each other motivated and informed to provide the best care for people.

Action Team 2

She called it a fireside chat. The female president of a large organic food company arranged it, and traveled far to meet us on that snowy winter's night. Warmed by our collective vision of *hope, health, and opportunity* for all, we pulled our chairs close to the glowing fire to share our inspiring stories.

We talked of things as diverse as rescuing wild mustangs, and returning them to vibrant health. We talked of teaching people in need how to start their own organic farms to feed themselves. We told of building a women's hospice, to help women regain their dignity and life purpose. We ended with stories of hope for children around the world, from the impoverished First Nations, to the abandoned children of war. We were offering food and loving support. Networking and teamwork make it possible. Good health gives us the energy to help others.

Action Team 3

Networking is people connecting with people to further their dreams. From early morning breakfasts, to late evening dinners, from women's groups, to mixed groups, business-networking meetings provide professional counsel, guidance, business expertise and friendship to help us manifest our dreams.

CAPS, the Canadian Association of Professional Speakers, is a favourite of mine. Speakers – many of them authors – gather to hone their skills and promote one another in business. For me, it is a tremendous forum for spreading good news – everything is available for us to make life-enhancing choices.

Networking connects people of like minds.

Watch for the synchronicity that inspires you when making your choices. It makes life so joyful. It often affirms or helps you focus your dream. Imagine my delight when I was drawn to sit beside Eva Marsh at a business-networking meeting and found out she was the author of a book called, '*Black Patent Shoes, Dancing With MS*'. Her story is one of 'unquenchable spirit', as she challenges all the beliefs and practices involved with this disease. How she comes to full recovery and what she has to teach us will astound you. When I first picked up Eva's book, and read the title, it wasn't just the topic of MS that caught my attention – dancing was also a metaphor for my mother's life, as well as her favourite activity. Her black patent dancing shoes sit proudly in my closet. Sometimes, I slip them on.

Over the years, my body and mind have awakened to a level of health and vitality I never thought possible. I don't even entertain the thought of illness anymore. In fact, my medicine cabinet has been empty for 14 years. Vital health starts with a strong intention, followed by informed choices, supported by friends and colleagues of like mind. With vibrant health as your foundation, you can choose the imprint you want to make in this lifetime.

You can be an Edge-Rider. Come to the Edge…

While it is often frightening to be like the bird that Victor Hugo described; "…that pausing in her flight awhile on boughs too slight, feels them give way beneath her and yet sings, knowing she has wings."

Know, too, that you have wings.

Biography For Carole Kent

Business Name: Edge-Rider International
Address: 1259 Dillon Road,
   Burlington, ON   L7M1R5
Telephone: (905) 336-7001
Email: ckent@cogeco.ca
Web Address: www.carolekent.com

Canadian Association of Professional Speakers Chapter:
   Hamilton: Professional Member

About Carole:
Carole Kent's focus is on wellness as the foundation for business success and personal   well-being. Carole believes vital health is possible for an entire lifetime. In her keynote speeches and workshop series, Carole uses humour and compassion to inspire audiences to 'Come to the Edge' – to look at habits or beliefs that may undermine their health and result in time lost, opportunities missed, and dreams shattered.

Through her membership in the Health Professionals Network, Cell Tech International and The Organic Farm, Carole has access to human resources, current research, and leading-edge strategies that support and promote healthy lifestyle choices. With joy and simplicity Carole coaches individuals in developing action plans that change one habit at a time, and guarantee a lifetime of physical energy and mental stamina.

Carole Kent is a graduate of Mc Master University and York University. She has 30 years experience as a teacher, educational consultant, and personal development and leadership trainer for school boards and businesses.

Journey to Wholeness

By: Audrey Pihulyk
Possibilities Network

Unravelling the past to move forward to the future

We all have a sponge inside that needs watering on a regular basis. This sponge represents our individuality, personhood, how we see ourselves, and is the basis of our self-esteem. The water that fills this sponge is the affirmation, acceptance, praise, and encouragement that we all need to live productive and joy-filled lives. Unfortunately, some may have been raised in dysfunctional families and, never really having their emotional needs met, are now living with a sense of 'something lacking'. Their sponges have been chronically dry, and now, as adults, they don't know how to ask for help in order to have their needs met. So, an inner ache remains that stems from years of emotional neglect. As an outcome of this, living in a co-dependent way becomes present in our relationships. It is at the core of addictive behaviour. It was at the core of my life.

The Awakening

It had been a wonderful time of travelling and camping with my family. We were in a quaint little place called Lyndon in the State of Washington. As we strolled own the street we stepped into a small bookstore. I was only two feet into the store when I saw it – the book that would change my life! Confessions of a Closet Eater, by Jackie Barrile.

At the time, I knew neither what drew me to the book, nor what impact it would have on my life – but later, as I read the book, MY AWAKENING began. It is clear that awakening comes when the pain of dysfunction is greater than the fear of change.

"Action and reaction, ebb and flow, trial and error, change – this is the rhythm of living. Out of our over-confidence, fear; out of our fear, clearer vision, fresh hope. And out of hope - progress."
                                                            -Bruce Barton

This powerful quote by Barton describes my awakening – a time when my entire being was spent, and I realized deep within that there had to come a change, as I could not go on.

As often happens, crisis precedes change. This change is the awakening that brings a stronger self. When you face a crisis of change, you may have thoughts such as mine:

> I thought, 'If I *go for the change, what about my identity that I have lived with all these years?* I thought, *'I will be a nothing, something to dread – the unknown!'*

These thoughts rushed through my mind, and took hold of my emotions, as I came to the realization that something had to be done. The Chinese character for crisis further illustrates this. It shows the very essence of crisis that brings change. When we embrace change, there is the danger of losing our identities brought about by the impact of change. But, glorious opportunities follow; to experience wholeness and to see the world through a different pair of eyes. This makes the risk worthwhile.

A Chinese Character for Crisis

Meaning Danger and Opportunity

The Roots of Change

I was raised in a rather authoritative home where there were no gray areas. My siblings and I were expected to live up to the expectations of our parents, whose desires were always for us to make them proud. As I look back now, it is clear how these aspects impacted me, and led to co-dependent behaviour as an adult.

Growing up, and even as a married adult with three healthy children, I often felt that there was a block somewhere in my chest. On the outside, I was healthy, happy, and a humourous person. However, little did anyone know the turmoil I felt within, which was a symptom of my lost identity. Something was amiss, but I didn't know how to fix the problem.

In her book, *Confessions of a Closet Eater,* Barrile writes about the emotional 'child' and the need to develop an emotional 'parent'. As I read, and began to understand the concept, I realized (to my horror) that I was still emotionally a child inside. Here I was, an adult on the outside, but not on the inside. How could this be? As I meditated on this for a period of time, I began to realize that it was true.

I had defined the world and my self-image from childhood experiences and perceptions that were based on the words and actions of the dysfunctional people in my young life. I thought that these people did what they did because of me. These misconceptions contributed to my low self-esteem, and therefore, my ultimate view of the world. Because of this, I had no emotional parent *within* to love, affirm, and nurture me. Instead, I was expecting others to meet my needs and bring me happiness. It was clear that things needed to change. So began my journey to wholeness, which was a journey into the unknown and over scary paths. The journey to discover the *real Audrey*, and to understand the crippling effects from years of being co-dependent, finally began. I began to realize that:

- I had been living in a co-dependent way in my life that led to my need to control others;
- as a result of early emotional bruising, I had desperately hung onto control;
- my little 'child within' was crying out for a 'parent' to love and affirm her;
- I needed to come to terms with how I viewed my body;
- acceptance and self-esteem are not dependant on someone else;
- I was no longer a victim, but could take the power over my own life, and
- giving up control and learning new ways is true power

Our Emotional House

We can compare life to an emotional house that has footings, a foundation, and a few stories. This emotional house of ours has been built since conception, either on a firm foundation or a weak one. As we take on the challenge of examining our emotional house, we begin to realize that important changes are needed to be made before we can travel on the road to recovery. The development of this house is closely related to the development of an emotional 'parent' within who can help us on our journey to wholeness.

Early in my journey, while facing the crisis of change, I began to listen to my 'child within'. My 'child' had a loud and accusing voice. It was the only voice that I had ever known, and it had been my identity until now. This was a scary time, fraught with doubts and fears. The cry within me was, *'If I make the change, what will I be like after…what will be the outcome…how will others see me…will they still love me?'*

People with addictive behaviours – whether it be to food, alcohol, drugs, or gambling – tend have a great deal of 'child' within. On my journey, there were two distinct aspects that I could identify. The first had a loud voice that spent its time accusing me with messages that said, *'How can you be so stupid?… no one will ever love you. You will never amount to anything!'* These accusations were imbedded in my mind, and had the voice of an authoritative parent. I grew up believing these accusations to be true, and so, had not developed a 'positive parent' within. Interestingly enough, the second part of the 'child' could not speak, it could only act. And, act it did. When the 'child' got fed up with the accusations, my addictions took over. Despair ran my life.

As many who have discovered freedom from addictions, it is critical to recognize the impact that these negative internal messages – or 'tapes' – have on your life. It helps to become quiet within, face and uncover the emotional bruising – the first step on your journey to wholeness. The awakening follows, and is a blessed opportunity to examine your life.

In my case, I examined my relationship with God, my birth family and present family, with my job, and even my life in general. After deciding that I wanted to live from inner wellness, my two-year process of awakening began. The statement:

You will know the truth, and the truth will set you free.

-The Bible

began to reverberate. I began to question what was really true about my life? I even had even begun to question what was truth.

If, for years, we live believing lies about ourselves, and of others, or wondering how to relate in the world, finding the truth to counteract the lies opens the door to recovery. To overcome the poor mental habits and low self-esteem brought about by such critical inner voices, we must recognize that these are distorted thoughts and, therefore, not true. We overcome them by talking back to them. Continuing to do so will reinforce the truth, and help us to feel better. At the same time, it boosts our self-esteem and sense of well-being. We must be willing to give up our old identities for the unknown to experience the release of exchanging addiction for freedom.

> *"Change is difficult, because the outcome is always uncertain. Nevertheless, change is a pre-requisite for growth, and it can make the difference between a dull and an exciting life."*
> *- Ken Hultman, from Making Change Irresistible*

It is a marvellous thing that, as we accept change and overcome the fear of the old, accusing tapes (the critical inner voice), the 'child within' becomes quieter and more peaceful. It then becomes easier to develop a new set of tapes – a gift from the emerging 'parent'.

While building on the foundation of our new emotional houses, we need to ask ourselves: *'Is there anyone I need to confront or forgive?' 'Are there any misconceptions or falsehoods that I need to let go of?'* We cannot avoid these issues. To face them now is to choose freedom. Not to face them rebuilds on the old foundations that we tore down. As much as we desire a new house, no construction can begin successfully until these tasks are carefully and lovingly completed.

Each of us needs to decide for ourselves what kind of houses we want to construct – how many stories, which rooms will be the largest, or most brightly decorated? This is an important step, because we will live in these new houses the rest of our lives. How can we make them homes instead of just houses? Understanding how this emotional angst makes itself real in our lives will help us construct new, healthy homes.

Indicators of Living with Co-dependence

As I moved forward in my journey, I began to realize that I had been relying on someone or something outside of myself for my happiness and fulfillment. Because of this mindset, in my daily interactions with my husband and children, and with others around me, I would react, rather than act. I felt passive, as though they were judging me, which then caused me to react, rather than act from my true self. I was dependant on others, not really knowing who I was inside. It was natural, then, to be passive, moved about by the attitudes and words of those around me, letting others have too much influence over my decisions. Because I had lived this way for so long, I would excuse it as 'just my way of being' – a sure way of opting out. It was the words of someone close to me telling me to *live the truth* which helped me take an honest look at my life. I realized what was going on. I had been expecting someone or something else to complete me! The following things were some of the ways of coping that I had developed that I knew I needed to address, and give up.

Control

Control was an issue in my life, mainly because I was controlled as a child, and, as an adult, I was struggling to have some kind of power, which then showed up as control. Yes, I was going to control something – even if it was only my eating. My deepest fear was that someone would take away my happiness, security, or self-worth, and then I would be subjected to more pain. Sometimes though, if we were controlled in our early lives, we continue to let others control us. We don't realize that we can break free. When our happiness is dependent on how others treat us and we, in turn, react, there is a pain that leaves us with difficulty in establishing truly meaningful and honest relationships. As I began to experience inner growth, and the emotional 'child within' began to develop into the 'parent' that I needed, my need for control became less of an issue.

The Need for Love

Deep in the heart of each one of us is the need to give and to receive love – the kind of love that has no expectations, does not hold back, but gives freely. Sometimes, as a result of our bruising, it is difficult to have our need for love met in a healthy manner. This may be partly due to the fact that the affirmation and unconditional love that we needed as a child was lacking, and now, we have love-shaped holes in our hearts. This hole can be described in various ways. Some describe it as a gnawing feeling, or even a kind of an emptiness that can be felt in the pits of their stomachs.

The love-shaped holes in our hearts can be a dilemma. How can we fill this void? It will take time. Yes, it can be a scary time, as the Chinese character shows – a time of both danger and opportunity. To begin to fill this void, and to break free, I developed a four-part plan:

- Step#1: Listening to the cries of my inner 'child'
- Step#2: Setting time aside to meditate and listen to the 'One' who knew me best
- Step#3: Examining my past and current life, and
- Step#4: Gathering the assistance of those I trusted for help and guidance.

These all worked in concert as I journeyed. The change was slow and painful, but definitely rewarding.

Living the Victim Role

Being the youngest of three children, and somewhat spoiled, I expected favour to follow me through life and, when it did not, I saw myself as a victim. I looked for someone to fix the problems, someone on whom to place the blame – after all, I felt powerless. Feeling like a victim left me confused and unable to accept responsibility for my actions. The following story reflects this:

> *The story is told of a man who was walking down a beach. A seagull flew over and 'dropped one' on his nose. He became so angry with the seagull that he reasoned within himself that, since the seagull did this to him, the seagull would have to get it off him as well. When he returned to his friends, they were repulsed and asked him to clean off his nose. The man refused to do so as he felt that the mess was entirely the seagull's fault.*
>
> *Later that night, his wife refused to have him sleep in the bed. He laid on the couch, lonely and dejected. His friends didn't want him and his wife had rejected him. All he could think of was, 'It's not my fault!'*
>
> *The next day, he went to work, and because he still refused to bathe, no one wanted to be near him. His thinking was that, if he bathed, his nose would have been clean, and the seagull would have gotten away with this unfair treatment. Things went from bad to worse. Clients refused to do business with him and he eventually was fired. His feeling was that his boss, co-workers and clients were all being unfair to persecute him this way. So now, homeless and without a job, he sits under an overpass, seeing himself completely blameless, but victimized by the world. And everyday, he looks up at the sky, knowing who is to blame.*
>
> *- Dr. James B. Richards from 'Co-dependent Christianity'*

Can you relate to this story? I know that I could. For so long, I had lived as a victim, seemingly powerless with what life brought my way, wallowing in self-pity. Seeing myself as a victim was reinforced when I *assimilated* hurtful situations. At the times when someone did or said something that hurt my feelings, I would naturally believe that it was true. I would even feel physical pain in my heart. Through trial and error, and over a period of time, I began to learn that the emotional and subsequent physical pain was the result of *my attaching* importance to what others said and did. As I began to develop more truth in my life, and to heal, I found strength in refusing to be hurt by the words and actions of others. Amazingly enough, the emotional and physical pain stopped.

Through these and other insights, my freedom began to unfold as I took a long, hard look at my life, and realized that only *I* had the power to change and move on. It was a scary time, giving up the only identity I had known all my life, and knowing that I would be taken in a new direction. There was the unknown of the journey ahead, not raw fear. I knew I was on the path to wholeness.

Body Image

If you are having problems with body image, you are not alone. Sometimes, learning to appreciate our bodies is a life-long mission. I spent years disliking my shape, trying to look like the fashion models, and hoping that others approved of my body shape.

Again, our childhoods play an important role in how we view our bodies. I remember those times in grade school, when I was teased about my round shape, and the many times I was chosen last for baseball. As children, we take these things to heart. These incidents play as tapes in our minds, and can have a profound long-term effect on our lives. Your mission and joy is to replace these tapes with affirming words, words of love to yourself that will help you to break free.

Building a New Inner Home

On my journey, I looked at the whole concept of co-dependency, and assimilated the knowledge I had learned to bring healing to my bruising. I built myself a new inner home with a firm foundation. As I travelled the journey to wholeness, my emotional 'child' had now become an adult, and I could choose the type of construction and decor of my new home.

My previous house was just that – a house, but not a home. Was I comfortable in it? No, but it was all I'd had and was the house that others helped me build – the house of my addictive behaviours. Now, I have built a strong, upright house that will be my new home – a home where others can come and visit, sit for a cup of tea beside the fire and tell me their stories. It is a place of refuge for others who too have experienced the storms of life, for those who want to make the journey, and experience the awakening, as I have.

I remember well systematically tearing down my old emotional house with its uncomfortable memories and lies that were built into the walls. I remember straightening the footings – painful but rewarding. I remember also putting up the walls. Those joists sure were heavy, but there were helpers. My home now has three stories, with beautifully decorated rooms. In fact, one of the rooms has a window that I like to open, and watch as the breeze plays with the curtain while I listen to the birds sing.

Yes, I remember the old house, now gone. What satisfaction I felt when I completed my new home, put on the shingles, and stretched the chimney toward the sky. Then, in a moment of triumph, I viewed the smoke of healing wafting from the chimney; a vivid sign of a new life within.

As I was building my home, I would often sit and look at a painting by Inuit artist, Benjamin Chee Chee. It is a stark picture of four geese in full flight, their wings outstretched and their long graceful bodies gliding through the air. As I sat on my couch, with my soul in turmoil, looking at the glorious freedom of the geese, there was a voice inside of me that spoke directly to my soul, *'Someday, you will be flying like them.'* And you know, I am!

What can I say – it has been a good journey, a time of fear, clarity, fresh hope and progress. I invite you to travel your journey to wholeness and experience your own awakening. Leave the old path behind, and walk into the new opportunities that await you. I leave you with this encouragement.

Go ahead, reach beyond your grasp!

Biography for Audrey Pihulyk

Business Name: Possibilities Network Inc.
Address: 8717 – 162 Street
Edmonton, Alberta   T5R 2M2
Telephone: (780) 484-2197
Fax: (780) 484-6630
Email: audrey@possibilitiesnetwork.com
Web Address: www.possibilitiesnetwork.com

Canadian Association of Professional Speakers Chapter:
Edmonton, Professional Member

About Audrey:
Audrey Pihulyk is a dynamic and humorous professional presenter, offering practical solutions to life's issues. Her motivating keynotes and interactive training sessions are described as inspiring and energizing, bringing value and lasting results. She works with associations and corporations to help them empower their people through maximizing their potential in the workplace. Audrey presents on topics such as stress, the value of humour, communication skills, team building, and women's issues.

Audrey is a syndicated columnist throughout Canada with her articles 'Winning Strategies for Life', and has authored a number of audiocassettes on related issues. She holds a certificate in Continuing Education from the University of Alberta, has designations from Toastmasters, is qualified in Myers-Briggs Type Indicator and has training in both voice and piano.

Audrey encourages you to 'Reach beyond your grasp'.

Maximize Living

By: Gayle Church
Stress and Wellness Solutions

Five tips to get more living out of life, and life out of living!

Inside each of us exists an infinite potential for living a fuller, more enriched life. Imagine how it would feel to realize that potential! It is my philosophy that each of us can take greater control over our own health and well-being than any other aspect of our lives. Through observation over the years, I've noticed that there are people who just get by in this life, and then, there are those who maximize living. What does it mean to maximize living? For years, I have lived my life on the basis of maximizing living. This may mean different things to different people, but for me, it means to *get more living out of life, and more life out of living.*

People today are already maxed out, burned out, and are merely surviving in life, and not thriving. When we think of people who live well, we often think in terms of financially well off. However, when I refer to people who live well, I am referring to people who live life well day-to-day, within their bodies, their hearts, and their minds. With the right tools, we can learn to live fuller, more meaningful enriched lives. These five tips for maximizing living can make the difference in enabling us to get more life out of living:

1. having a goal in life,
2. living in the moment,
3. managing your stress,
4. maximizing your nutrition, and
5. living a more balanced life within

It's often easier for people to settle for what's barely working, than to fix a problem and deal with the discomfort of making positive changes in their lives. For those of you who feel you don't have time or energy to change, consider the alternative of not changing the way you are currently living. Is this really how you envisioned your life would be? Time is always going to be a reason for not incorporating new and better habits. But, when you have a deep, burning desire for a healthier, happier, less stressful life, we will find the time.

Tip #1: Having a Goal in Life

> *"There is one elementary truth, the ignorance of which kills*
> *countless ideas and suspended plans: that the moment when one*
> *definitely commits oneself, then providence moves too. All sorts of*
> *things occur to help one that would never have otherwise*
> *occurred. A whole stream of events issues from the decision,*
> *raising to one's favour all manner of unforeseen incidents and*
> *meetings and material assistance which no man could have*
> *dreamt would have come his way."*
>
> *- W. H. Murray, Himalayan explorer*

People who maximize living are successful goal setters. They are the
ones who find health, wealth, and happiness. These are some of the benefits
of having goals:

- Goal setting can pull you through the darkest times, when life looks
  empty and dark.
- Goals have the ability to keep you going. Even when you don't have
  the energy, you still have the *drive* for the goal.
- Excitement and enthusiasm for life can come from goals.
- Goals can offer hope, a chance, and a reason for living.
- Goals can help reduce stress. Like the quote above implies, all sorts of
  things begin to happen when you properly set a goal, allowing
  providence to help in unforeseen ways. It's like getting extra help and
  resources, with less stress.
- Goal setting can save you time and energy. It makes less work of what
  you are trying to accomplish.

Goals don't have to be difficult to accomplish, if you're using the right system.
When you stop struggling so hard, and let go, it helps reduce stress and worry
over *how* things will be accomplished. When you discover the *natural laws* of
goal setting, you will begin to enjoy a more rewarding life.

> *"The dream you dream shall live in your memory, a delight that*
> *will never stale. It will be your inspiration for years to come."*
>
> *- Felice Benuzzi*

Take a Moment to Reflect on Goals: What one 'small' goal could you set, and easily achieve, that would make a positive difference in your life?

_____

_____

_____

Tip #2: Living in the Moment

> *"Drink life. Live each moment with passion."*
> *-Wei Chen, Broadcaster*

Does the following sound familiar to you?:

> *As I sat lounging in the sun on the chaise at the cottage, I found it difficult to really relax. I pondered over the things I should be doing at the house – things that don't really need my attention. They aren't urgent. They are just so-called 'productive' things that I feel I should or could be doing. Then, I spent time worrying about the things I had coming up in the future – things I had to prepare for the upcoming fall sessions – work I should get started on soon but not too soon. I found it difficult to sit comfortably, relax, and enjoy the moment. Each time I was at the cottage, I felt more stress. I worried about things I should be doing back at the house. When working at home, I'd think of how nice it would be to have time to relax at the cottage, and walk along the beach. I can't win.*

I realized that the very moment I was living in, I wasn't enjoying it as much as I could or should. In my mind I was living in another place and time. How could I miss out on watching the kids play on the beach, or the very beauty of nature that surrounded me as I lay resting in my chaise? Can you imagine missing out on enjoying a truly enjoyable day at the beach? This pattern unnerved me for years. Then, it stopped. I stopped. That was over 12 years ago. I decided that I have a right, the need, and deserve to take time to refuel my mind, body, and spirit – not only for me, but also for the benefits my family would receive from me being a happier, more relaxed person.

When I finally made the transformation to living in the moment, everything became so axiomatic, so very much more meaningful and alive with abundance. Time seemed to stand still. I became very present in my own life, and began experiencing all that I had been given – the good and the bad – but it was my experience, right here and now.

Have you ever had an experience like that, where you have been involved in some event, and you've had other things on your mind, and you feel you shouldn't really be there, that perhaps you have other things you could be doing? Depending on the situation, decide what's best for you. Two questions you can ask yourself to help you decide in a situation like that are, 1) is this the best use of my time?, and 2) is this moving me towards my goal?

> **The past does not exist; the future does not exist. All that exists is right here, right now, this very moment in time.**

Suppose we divided time into three equal parts: the past, the present, and the future, each part representing one-third. Now, suppose you spend a lot of time living in and worrying about the past things that happened last week, or last month, at work. That would represent one-third of unnecessary worry and stress. Now, suppose you also spend time worrying about the future, for example, how you're going to get your son to his play-off game at the end of the month because you have to be out of town, or, perhaps all the errands and running around you have to do on the weekend? That equals another one-third of excess stress you don't really need to deal with at this very moment. Your total *extra* stress is up to two-thirds.

Now, consider living in the moment. As you live and work in the moment of now, what is it for you that needs your attention? What is it that you may be worried or stressed about? For example, if it's thinking of how you're going to make that deadline by 4:00 p.m. today, this represents another one-third of your total stress and worry. If you tend to live in all three areas – the past, present and future – the total amount of stress you experience equals 100 percent. But, for people who choose to live in the moment, they have only one-third of the stress to deal with, compared to those who live in all three (past present and future). Wouldn't it be great if you could reduce your stress and worry by two-thirds, simply by learning to live in the moment? Time is valuable. When it's gone, it can't be replaced. Live each moment with passion. Maximize living.

"Yesterday is a cancelled cheque.
Tomorrow is a promissory note.
Today is the only cash you have, spend it wisely."
– Author Unknown

Take a Moment to Reflect on Living in the Moment: What one thing will you do, today, to slow down and experience more of living in the moment?

_____

_____

_____

Tip #3: Managing Your Stress

"Life is sweet, you know. I've never met a person who really
wanted to die. We want to live."
– *Dr. Marius Barnard, Heart Surgeon*

Are you aware that heart disease and stroke are the #1 causes of death of Canadian women? (based on the Heart and Stroke Association). Stress has been linked to heart disease but stress is not the culprit. It is mis-managed stress that can hurt, and even kill. While health care costs associated with heart disease and stroke are in the billions of dollars, the human costs of these diseases to Canadian families are – immeasurable. Experts on stress tell us we should never underestimate the toll that stress takes on our bodies. Studies now show that as much as 80% of all illnesses are stress related. The stress response negatively alters and changes what happens within our bodies. These changes include: the constriction of our blood vessels; speeding up our heart rates and respiration; increasing the clotting factors in our blood streams; and suppressing our immune systems, thus making us more vulnerable to disease.

<u>Top 10 Reasons Why Stress Management is Beneficial</u>
1. Reduces risk of heart disease.
2. Improves the quality of your life.
3. Releases stress and tension.
4. Prevents and heals physical problems.
5. Improves your sleep.

6. Reduces memory loss.
7. Contributes to emotional mastery.
8. Manages pain.
9. Contributes to graceful aging.
10. Improves mental and physical performance.

Steps to Successful Stress Management

Step #1: Acknowledge the need for change. Change begins with the desire. When you have the desire to change, fueled with the proper motivation, your change will be more successful, long term.

Step #2: Identify the sources of your stress. Take time to become aware of your environment and discover what, and who, are stressful for you. Also, be aware of what time of day is most stressful for you – when and where you get stressed.

> *The most beneficial coping skills are mind-body techniques.*

If you're stressed by time, and that is a problem for you, think about developing better time management skills. Perhaps you need help saying 'no', more often. Develop new assertive skills. Try role-playing with a friend. However, the most beneficial coping skills are mind-body techniques. Examples are techniques such as meditation, proper relaxation, and guided imagery.

The reason these work so well is because they address not only the physical symptoms of our health, but also the framework of attitudes and behaviours that surround the symptoms and diseases caused by stress. A study conducted at the Stress Reduction Clinic at the University of Massachusetts Medical Center, showed that there was a 25% reduction of physical symptoms over an eight-week period of intense stress-reductions training, and a 32% reduction in psychological symptoms such as anger and depression.

Managing the stress is your life is one of the most vital skills for success, no matter how you define success. Don't look for excuses of why you don't have time for managing your stress. Look for alternatives and the costs of not managing your stress. Sooner or later, it will catch up with you, and you will find the time, but it won't be at a time of your choice. Your body will make that choice for you.

Take a Moment to Reflect on Managing Your Stress: What do you sense is the cost of mismanaged stress to you and your family emotionally, physically, and financially? What one thing could you do 'today' to reduce your stress?

_____

_____

_____

Tip #4: Maximizing Nutrition

Every day, we make choices about our health, whether we realize it or not.

Because stress takes such a toll on our minds and bodies, and rapidly depletes the nutrients we have in our bodies, we need to maximize our nutrition to replace lost nutrients. In today's society, it becomes increasingly difficult to ensure healthy eating. We have much more food, but much less nutrition. We have more diet and fitness products, and more unfit people. We have more medicines, but less health.

The most important thing you can learn is to accept responsibility for your health and well-being. You have complete control over this area of your life. It's about choices. You can either be a pro-active participant in your health, or a reactive participant. A person who wishes to maximize living will choose to be a pro-active participant, one who works on prevention, rather than a reactive person who works on fixing his/her failing health due to disease.

Health encompasses the whole being; the mind, the body, and the spirit. The very essence that everything we think, say, and do, affects our health. We need to feed the body at a cellular level to repair damages done by stress, as well as for better health, energy, fuel, and vitality. Think of your health as a bank account. Everytime we eat healthy and exercise, we make a deposit into your health account. Every time you release stress, you make a deposit. Each time you smoke, you make a withdrawal. Each time you drink alcohol, and eat junk food, you're making a withdrawal. Every time you experience a lot of stress, think of it as making huge withdrawals on your health account. Relaxation and good sleep are deposits.

Anti-oxidant vitamins as well as calcium and magnesium should be included in your diet to enhance your immune system while under stress. And, these are vital nutrients that can help against heart disease, and need to be replaced regularly. In fact, our bodies often requires *twice the normal amount of nutrients when we are under stress.* We cannot continue to make withdrawals without making regular deposits. If we make more withdrawals than deposits, our health accounts will be bankrupt. That's when we experience serious illnesses and setbacks in our health. The biggest health complaint of women is fatigue and lack of energy, and the reason is that their bank accounts are mentally and physically overdrawn, and need some healthy, nutritional deposits to help them cope.

Develop the habit of maximizing nutrition. It is not an easy task to cook and prepare meals the way our parents used to. It appears that, in today's society, the quest for eating is not necessarily nutrition, but how fast it can be prepared, and will it be tasty and filling? Keep in mind that foods do not contain the same quality of nutrients as they used to years ago. We have more manufactured foods than ever before. We have nutrient depleted soils, increased processing and shipping, exposure to bright lights in the store – all of which deplete the nutrient levels. So what is a person to do to build up the nutritional part of their health account?

Building Your Nutritional Health Account

One option is to cook and prepare your meals that are as healthy as possible to retain nutrients. Eat more raw fruits and vegetables than you're used to. Eat more home-made lunches, and healthy snacks. Part of the key to this option is planning. Set time aside to plan your meals and your healthy snacks.

Another option for building your health account is to use food supplements. Incredibly few women are aware that one of the easiest and best ways to have better health is to supplement their diets. It's not about replacing the food we eat. Rather, it's about supplementing, enhancing, what we are already eating. All it takes is one minute a day. But, keep in mind, not all supplements are created equal. Consider only the highest quality all-natural food supplements, backed by clinical research and testing*.
(* Seek advice from a trained nutrition consultant).

Most of us deny our vulnerability, and even our mortality. When we acknowledge the consequences of our actions, it becomes easier to make sensible decisions, and take responsibility. Those who do not take time now for better health will quite likely have to find time to recover from disease. Which one do you think you would be better at coping with – *prevention, or cure?* Your health is one of your most vital assets. Remember, you can be a pro-active participant or a reactive participant when it comes to your health – the choice is yours.

Take a Moment to Reflect on Maximizing Nutrition: Ask yourself this question; 'If I continue with my health habits as I am, what will my health be like in 10 years? Will I have enough health to live on? What 'small step' could I take today to improve my nutrition?'

_____

_____

_____

_____

Tip #5: Live a More Balanced Life from Within

> *"The rewards of living a balanced life are filled with riches of*
> *every kind. However having an unbalanced life has its reward*
> *too—but sometimes the price is too high."*
>   *– Author Unknown*

Life begins within. Balance begins at the centre, within. The concept of balancing your life from an inside-out approach is gaining in popularity. Still, most people try to work on everything from outside their lives. When we live more balanced lives within, it overflows into our relationships, our work, our health and our successes. *As within, so without.*

Women Have the Most to Gain

Faced with unique challenges within our bodies, from the onset of our first menses to the last cycle of menopause, the benefits of inner balance to women's physical and mental health is immense. Women have the most to gain by living a more inner balanced life. The ability to maintain equilibrium within the mind and body is vital to women's health and self-preservation. When the mind, body, and spirit are in balance, we often find that the rest of our lives reflect that balance, and our whole life balance becomes more natural.

As a yoga teacher and mind-body stress relief facilitator, I know the value of balance and harmony within the body. Studies and research have proven the importance of inner balance. When the mind and body are in balance, we have a greater ability to restore harmony within the body, at both the cellular level as well as in the mind. Seek inner balance through practices that produce the *relaxation response*, like meditation. According to the Joan Borysenko, Ph.D., meditation can reduce common stress related ailments; from high blood pressure and headaches, to insulin-dependent diabetes and asthma. In her book, *'A Woman's Book of Life'*, Joan Borysenko states *"the fact is that almost any illness, no matter its cause, can be worsened by stress and improved by methods that restore us to inner balance"*.

Tips and Techniques

Studies have proven that at least 80% of illness and disease is stress related. The relaxation response is nature's balancing act against stress-related illness and disease. The relaxation response is not a technique. It is a series of changes that occur internally when the mind and body are balanced, tranquil, and in harmony. The goal is to elicit the relaxation response by using any proven mind-body techniques. The physiology of the relaxation response is very different than simply resting, or watching television.

Here are some scientific findings from research on the benefits of the relaxation response. In the book, *Healing Mind, Healthy Woman*, by Alice Domar, Ph.D., and Henry Dreher, they refer to a study conducted on 33 menopausal women, who experienced hot flashes. This study was conducted by Judith Irvin, Ph.D. and the author, Alice Domar, Ph.D. Their findings indicated a 50% decrease in the frequency and the intensity of hot flashes when these menopausal women elicited the relaxation response.

The technique we use is less important. What is important is the end result, eliciting the relaxation response. When asked by my clients which method works the best, I inform them that the one they enjoy, and will do on a regular basis, is the best method. This is where you will find results.

Techniques:

- Diaphragmatic breathing
- Meditation
- Repetitive prayer
- Various types of deep relaxation
- Guided imagery and
- Yoga

Tips:

- Choose one you enjoy doing
- Do it at the same time, daily/weekly, to build the habit
- Do it without expectations

- Do it in a relaxed manner, not rushed
- Consider using relaxation audio-tape at work, during lunch.

The key to balance is to constantly strive to re-balance when you are out of balance. That is where your strength lies. By becoming more balanced, and centered, you have greater abilities to cope with the realities of the day. When the mind, body, and spirit are in harmony, it shows in your relationships, your work and your health. The time has never been better to begin living a more balanced life from within.

Take a Moment to Reflect on Living a More Balanced Life from Within: What part of your body could benefit 'most' from living a more balanced life within? What 'small' step could you take to live a more balanced life within?

_____

_____

_____

In as much as we don't think that we have choices, we really do. We have more control over our own health and well-being than we realize. Every day, we make a choice about our health, whether we realize it or not. Regardless of your choices, each minute of the day, every new sunrise, is an opportunity for change – a second chance. The question is, will you? Will you continue living as you have done in the past, or will you maximize living? Inside each and everyone one of us exists an infinite potential to get more living out of life, and more life out of living. If I could inspire you to do one thing, it would be to connect with your deepest desires, and maximize living!

> *There is a tale about a youngster who wanted to confound a certain wise man. He captured a butterfly and held it in his closed hands. He said to the wise man: "I have something here. In your wisdom, tell me if it is alive or dead." The sage knew that if he said the creature was alive, the lad would crush it, before opening his hands. If he said it was dead, the youth would open his hands and let it flutter away. The wise man said, "The answer is in your hands".*

> *And so it is with you and your life. The choice is yours.*
> *The answer is in your hands.*

Information on nutrition in this chapter is from the following resources:

Ann Louse Gittleman   Super Nutrition for Menopause

Phyllis Balch, CNC,   Prescription for Nutritional Healing,
and James Balch,   3rd Edition

Dr. Steve Chaney,   Research Scientist, and Dr. Chris Jensen,
      VP Shaklee Health Science

Biography for Gayle Church

Business Name: Gayle Church Stress and
Wellness Consulting
Address: 1 Marvin Drive
St. Catharines, Ontario
L2M 1X6
Telephone: (905) 934-7211
Fax: (905) 937-9004
Email: Gayle.Church@sympatico.ca
Web Address: www.gaylechurch.com

Canadian Association of Professional Speakers Chapter:
Hamilton

About Gayle:

Gayle is an award winning Toastmaster, speaker, mind and body stress-relief facilitator/trainer, and consultant specializing in stress management. For over 16 years, she has inspired and motivated individuals to reach their potential for health and success.

She empowers organizations and individuals to transform their intentions into reality. Audiences come away with practical, proven strategies for improved health, performance, and success. As a consultant, Gayle is committed to working closely with clients, in order to co-create practical solutions with results-oriented techniques.

Gayle is a graduate of the Hatha & Raja Yoga Studies, in Toronto, Ontario. She resides in the Niagara Peninsula, where she conducts stress management, relaxation, and yoga programs.

Her Goal: To help you achieve your goals.

"Wisdom is the outcome of listening to, trusting,
and following intuition over and over again."
                                    - *Kathy Glover Scott*

Passionately Alive
With Purpose

By: Tammy Adams
Turning Point

Living your life and your career with honesty.

Life is not static. As Canadians, we experience a change of seasons moving from fall, to winter, to spring, to summer, and back to fall. For many, fall represents an end as the flowers die, the animals hibernate, and the birds migrate to a warmer climate. We feel a sense of closure. We appear to rest through the winter season, preparing for spring. It brings a freshness, a rebirth, and a renewed sense of purpose. Summer is a time for growth, and *union with purpose*, a reason for being. It is the meaning of this existence that I wish to explore.

What is purpose? How do we make the connection? How do we find meaning in what we do? How do we live passionately?

> 'Living your life with purpose', means, 'living your life with integrity'. It is being true to yourself, true to your values, and true to your needs at all times.

For the longest time, I believed purpose and mission were interchangeable with career goals. As a career coach, my understanding was that if you were going to spend 40 plus hours at a job, then you should really be sure you were in the right line of work, with the right people, in the right environment. I still believe your career choice should be a well-planned goal, however, it is not a destination. In my own career, I have changed roles several times. I have been a waitress, an early childhood educator, a college professor, a resource consultant, a speaker, a corporate trainer, a career coach, a writer – only to name a few.

Each change was motivated by the excitement of a challenge, the opportunity to learn, and the chance to apply past skills in a new situation. With the shifts in today's workplace, with the reality of four or five career changes per lifetime, you are being provided these same opportunities for choice, and change. You have the chance to be in charge of your career. It should be a process of evolution where you are able to grow, and develop your talents, and share them with others, in as many places as you choose.

As mentioned earlier, I believed *purpose and mission* were interchangeable with career. However, the real truth is that living with purpose includes – but is not exclusive to – your work. You can actually live your life with purpose every day! Not too long ago, I delivered a keynote with a theme of 'women and balance'. As I spoke, the following happened.

> *My focus was on the concept of finding happiness in everyday moments. A woman in the crowd nodded her head in agreement. This was a defining moment for me, as I have known this woman for over 25 years, and have enormous respect for this lady of maturity. She has always held her head high, generously given all she has to those in need, and demonstrated a positive attitude, no matter the challenges.*
>
> *When I speak of challenges I know she has had many: she delivered her first child alone, while her husband served overseas (the baby would be almost one and one-half years before he would meet his father); she was a nurse at a time when there was little respect for her profession; she has buried two sons and one husband; and has lived her life with a mentally-challenged daughter (whom she describes as her greatest gift).*
>
> *I never knew her secret of survival, until that day. As she smiled, and nodded, in agreement, at the mention of those moments every day that provide the comfort and connection we are all looking for, I understood her strength.*

Living your life with purpose is the same. If you approach your career and your daily encounters with others from within, you are able to put your mark on the world in a meaningful way.

Creating a Meaningful Existence

To find the harmony you crave in your life, two things must occur:

1) you will need to become more aware of who you are, and
2) have a sense of what you want.

These two things need to be present, before you can make the shift. It takes courage to create a meaningful existence. The rewards are enormous…as are the risks. Before you begin the process of self-discovery, I caution you, as this will be a challenging experience. It takes a lot of work and a strong commitment to see this part of your journey through to the end. Taking charge of your career path, and finding what will truly make you happy is an enormous undertaking, and, in the end, is well worth the effort.

The clues to your career/life direction may have already presented themselves to you. Often, we are too distracted by life's demands to notice. To provide you some clues, answer the following questions. There is space below to record your responses.

- Where do you like to spend your free time?
- What song lyrics have 'spoken' to you?
- What section of the bookstore do you find yourself attracted to?
- What do you dream about (day or night)?
- When was the last time you listened to a hunch?
- Why have you resisted some opportunities?

_____

_____

_____

_____

_____

_____

_____

Identifying Resistance

As you consciously begin to live a life of purpose, you must be willing to take full responsibility for your life. Consciously means being aware of, and taking responsibility for, the decisions you make daily. This means going back to the beginning, dissecting the lessons of your past, and discovering where your beliefs about life had started. You need to keep the patterns that have worked, and release the ones that no longer serve you in a positive way. Unlearning lessons that have created barriers, and have kept you stuck in the same pattern for years, is essential to your moving forward.

When you accept ownership of your life and your choices, you gain a new inner strength.

> **Personal power is important to individual achievement, and your greatest power is your capacity to choose.**

By giving yourself permission to ponder and reflect on questions such as, *"Why am I here?"* and *"What is my passion?"*, you open the door to the possibility of success, and spiritual balance.

Individuals exploring their personal sense of purpose can experience depression, or feel despondent. Some identified reasons for this internal conflict are that a person:

- does not believe that she deserves it,
- does not believe it is possible,
- allows her common sense 'head' to over rule her creative 'heart',
- finds that the need for adventure is overruled by the comfort of the familiar,
- believes the past dictates the future,
- associates change with risk, and risk with failure.

For many, the joy of following a dream puts them in opposition with family values. If you allow it, this contradiction will be reinforced by every mistake you have ever made. This creates support for your existing paradigm. It will be important to identify the source of these values. Are they yours, or have they been inherited from someone else?

Mapping Who You Are

Once you have identified your resistance, you will need to continue the process by documenting your personality. For example:

Values: In the world of work, the common sources of discomfort are when the personal values of your employer and yourself do not align. Can you list what is important to you, such as those beliefs that you would stand for regardless of the consequences?

_____

_____

_____

_____

Your likes and dislikes: Can you list those things that energize you, and those activities that appear to drain you, shortly after you begin them?

_____

_____

_____

_____

Skills: What are the natural skills, and abilities, that others compliment you for – with or without formal education?

_____

_____

_____

_____

Needs: What are your personal needs in the area of rewards? What do you need in order to continue on a project: recognition, autonomy, money, etc.?

_____

_____

_____

_____

Learning Style: How are you most comfortable learning? Do you like to be shown, be provided a manual for a more self-directed approach? Are you hands-on learner? Do you prefer a group setting, etc.?

_____

_____

_____

_____

Once you have painted your portrait, you will then need to study the picture, and see if you can see the patterns. Finally, you will need to set goals, and map out a plan in order to reach them, remembering to remain open to suggestions and options along the way. (For a more detailed approach, you will find the steps clearly outlined in my new book, *Bring Yourself to Work, and Enjoy the Work You Choose*, available at http://www.career-lifeskills.com.)

Career Development is a Process

Developing your career is a creative process. It is about evolving, growing, and being open to opportunities. It is extremely important to remember that this is a continual process of learning. You will never remember everything the first time around. You are constantly adding new skills and abilities to your repertoire. Through this, you will gain an understanding of how remarkable you are. This includes experiencing the 'bad' as well as the 'good'. If you do not own the negative, it will own you!

As a child, I always wanted to be a teacher, a nurse, or a secretary. These professions include helping others, education, communication, and nurturing. Through reviewing my career path, it is clear that these characteristics exist in everything I have done to date. As a child, you knew your direction. This does not mean that, as a child, if you felt you would be a nurse, then that is what should be today. What is important is exploring what it was about being a nurse that appealed to you. This will provide you with very strong clues about your personal passion. For example, nurses help people, they are front line workers, they interact with people, and they are part of a team. These are elements that you will need to find in your life work.

Becoming conscious, taking personal responsibility for yourself, and for your career, your attitudes, and your personal health is a whole new way of being for many people. Make a decision to change your thoughts, words, and actions to match where you see yourself. This new level of consciousness will allow you to find satisfaction within yourself, no longer relying on external sources of praise and recognition. Don't expect a 'smooth ride', for you will experience both highs and lows. Obstacles are part of the journey. But, if you can remember that both are temporary, you will be up to the challenge.

Moving to Action

When your awakening happens isn't important. But, once you begin the search, the 'status quo' will be hard to maintain. The restlessness that began your quest will continue – until you take action. What can you do to prepare for action?

- **Don't be too serious**. Don't become a prisoner of the process.
- **Put your house in order**. Making any kind of career change will set you back financially, even if it is only for a short period of time. You either have to prepare yourself financially for a smaller paycheck, or you need to prepare yourself mentally for working two or more jobs until you reach your intended salary.
- **Surround yourself with positive people**. Don't be discouraged if those closest to you don't understand your career direction. After all, this is your dream…not theirs. Accept this, and find support with those individuals who will encourage you to achieve your goal.
- **Associate with 'like-thinking' people**. When people think the same, there is the strong possibility their thoughts will form a reality.
- **Build your network system**. Join a social group, take up a sport, or attend conferences. Meeting new people can be a frightening experience, but if you begin in places where you are comfortable, it provides a great place to practice.
- **Look for the lesson**. Breakdowns are those times when fear seems to overcome us, leaving us depressed, and despondent. The more frightened you become, the closer you are to making new, and exciting things happen. A lot of energy is wasted in denial. Be honest with yourself, and use that energy more productively. For some, it may be necessary to secure professional counselling to deal with these issues, and put them to rest.
- **Take some courses**. This is particularly helpful if you haven't been in a classroom setting for a long period of time. This not only prepares you mentally for learning, but it will demonstrate how much fun learning can be.
- **Read**. Read whatever you can find. Soon, you will be aware of the literature choices you are making, and the pattern to your choices.
- **Stop blaming others**. When you blame others for the situation you find yourself in, this gives away your power. Accept the fact that you cannot change the behaviour of others, but you can control the manner in which you react to certain situations
- **Change your perception**. If you believe you can't find a career where you will enjoy your work, YOU WON'T. Believe in abundance, not scarcity.
- **Become passionate about this pursuit**. In pursuing your 'dream job', thoughts and words are not enough. You must be committed to finding

the answer to what you truly want to do, and then give yourself to achieving it.

- **Document what you have done in the past.** This includes writing down what you have learned from it, what you liked, what you disliked, etc.
- **Be very clear with your message.** Others can't help you if they don't know where you're going. For that matter, you can't help yourself if you don't know where you're heading.
- **Don't be trapped by old survival tricks.**
- **Apply Newton's Law:** every action has an equal and opposite reaction. Positive thoughts must replace negative thoughts.
- **Take this one step at time.**
- **Understand you have choices.**
- **Signal a change.** Create a new image for yourself. Get a new hairdo, or buy some new clothes.
- **Enlist the assistance of a coach.** This is someone who will keep you on track, and provide you with the tools you need to discover your true talents.
- **Create strategic alliances.** You can take your career further and faster by building partnerships with those who either complement your skills, or balance your areas of weakness.
- **Give back.** Co-operation is the natural law of nature.
- **Look for the positive in your angst.** Don't continue to suffer.

Being Aware of the Void

As you re-evaluate your direction, you may find yourself in what some have described as the void – the nothing. It is when you seem to be looking for something, and nothing appears. You feel like you have hit a wall, stalled, become blocked. Don't be discouraged. Sometimes, you simply need to be still, and quiet for a while. As you release old patterns, you are, in fact, *transforming*. This can be viewed as a period of transition. As you move forward, you may need to grieve the past, and release it, in order to make room for the future.

I caution you not to try to find all the answers, for some questions don't have answers. Not everything can or will be explained. This should be a brief time of reflection, and reassessment. Here are some survival techniques for this time period:

- Be open to opportunities that come your way, even those you hadn't thought of.

- Take advantage of self-development opportunities.
- Be aware of repeated messages from a variety of sources.
- Reassess your existing belief system, and identify areas that need to be changed.
- Be clear on the feelings you want.
- Repeat goals several times a day (especially before falling asleep), but surrender the need to know how they will happen.
- Use this time to process, and sort thoughts you have been too busy to understand.
- Be receptive to an energy larger than yourself.
- Enjoy the time to yourself. Don't resist or feel you should be doing something.
- Begin a journal of what others say to you, and new people you meet… is there a message?
- Clean your office and home, and get rid of the clutter
- Don't be critical – accept it, and feel what it brings

Living a life of purpose, or finding a fulfilling career, at times, may seem to present conflicting messages. If you are new to this process, you can become confused and overwhelmed quickly. Try to think of it as a road trip. For example, today you will travel from Paris, Ontario to London, Ontario. You know that you have the option of taking Highway 401, or Highway #2, or a number of side roads. You know that you are heading to London, but you cannot view your destination from Paris. Along the way, you may see a bald eagle, there may be a car accident, you could have car trouble, you may arrive early, it could be a beautiful sunny day, or cloudy and overcast. *You understand that you have no control over what could happen on the way, but you trust that you will arrive.*

That is how you live a life of purpose. That is why a life of purpose has so many times been identified as a journey. You have the ability to choose a place you would like to visit, explore, experience, learn, share, and then move on to your next adventure. (Stopovers may vary from individual to individual.)

A single profession or career should not define your life work. You are not measurable by tangible means, but rather by feelings and personal rewards. You and your life purpose cannot be placed into a compartment and labeled FULFILLING. Your ability to meet your needs through your career, however, provides you with limitless options. Rather than search outside yourself for the answer you are seeking, relax, and look within. Choose to be yourself, each and every day, both professionally and personally. Take the time to check once in a while, to make sure that you are on target. Is your energy level high? Are you still happy with what you are doing? If the answer has changed, then you need to change. You have choices. You are not locked in. Your career choice is not permanent.

A life of purpose is about living your life to its fullest. It is not a single moment of truth, where suddenly, everything becomes permanently clear. It is about identifying your gifts, and knowing your strengths, and what your contribution can be, so that you can enjoy every opportunity along the way. While I visited 'the nothing' this past summer, I looked for the lesson I was learning as I released the past and moved forward yet again. I needed to be comfortable with not knowing what was next. I had to learn to trust myself, and know that what I was doing was right for me. I discovered that 'the nothing' isn't such a bad place to be, after all!

Biography for Tammy Adams

Business Name: Turning Point:
Professional Speaking and Consulting
Address: 23 Garden Crescent,
Paris, Ontario N3L 3T3
Telephone: (519) 442-0789
Fax: (519) 442-4303
Email: tammyadams@yourturningpoint.com
Web Address: www.yourturningpoint.com

Canadian Association of Professional Speakers Chapter:
Hamilton, Professional member

About Tammy:
Tammy Adams, author, professional speaker and trainer, has a unique ability to connect with and captivate an audience. Her upbeat energy, natural empathy, and professional edge are second to none. She has spent 20 years in the field of education while continuing to expand her own personal horizons. Tammy's personal and career paths are living proof that life experiences can be a powerful tool for transformation. In her presentations, she always leads by example, pulling from real-life experiences, and delivering life-changing words of inspiration, courage, and wisdom.

In her role as a seminar leader, Tammy delivers entertaining, performance-oriented solutions to unleash the natural strengths and talents of your existing team. She has developed a number of 'Making Diversity Work' solutions to harness individual uniqueness.

Tammy has enjoyed the bulk of her career in the field of education, as a childhood educator, a college professor, a program coordinator for a secondary school-to-work program, and a certified True Colors facilitator.

Books by Tammy:
Bring Yourself to Work, 2002

"While we have the gift of life, it seems to me the only tragedy is
to allow part of us to die – whether it is our spirit,
our creativity, or our glorius uniqueness."

- Gilda Radner

If You Can't Make Waves, Make Ripples

By: Janet Christensen
Unlimiting Potential

Personal leadership means knowing that everything counts.

Mother Teresa, Terry Fox, Adolph Hitler, Saddam Hussein, Rosa Parks, Charles Manson, Dr. Roberta Bondar, and You. What do all of these people have in common? They are all leaders. All of these people have a far-reaching effect beyond their direct personal impact, beyond what they see or know and, in some cases, beyond their own lifetimes. All of these people demonstrate that *everything counts*. We are talking about personal leadership, which is the personal impact that each of us has, whether or not we are aware of it. Are you making choices in life so you have the type of personal impact that you desire? If not, are you *really* making an impact? The extent of the impact of our personal leadership is our choice.

The notion that you are in such illustrious (and even infamous) company as this list of people, may strike you as strange. You may not see yourself as a leader; however, do not make the mistake of thinking that you cannot possibly be a leader. Each of us is a leader by virtue of the fact that 'everything counts'. Some people long for fame and notoriety, and may or may not get it; most people are content to live their lives on a less conspicuous level. Some people do not seek fame, yet

> *The extent of the impact of our personal leadership is our choice.*

it comes to them. Rosa Parks refused to give up her seat on a bus because she was physically fatigued, and tired of segregation in the southern United States. She had no idea that her brave, solitary act would play such an integral role in the American civil rights movement, and propel her into the history books. Terry Fox had no idea that his run across Canada to raise awareness and money for cancer research would leave a lasting legacy that continues on today, to inspire millions of people and raise millions of dollars. It is estimated that Mother Teresa personally connected with 80,000 people during her lifetime; yet, millions throughout the world know her name and work. This is known as…

The Ripple Effect

Water covers about 75% of the earth. It is a necessity of life, and a life force. Water continually shapes our world, and its impact is felt when there is too much of it, too little of it, and even when it is in a balanced supply. A tsunami (or giant tidal wave) strikes with relentless force. It leaves in its wake death and destruction. Its effects are felt far beyond where it hits. Waves can be dramatic and sweeping, creating change and constant transformation. Ripples are gentle and subtle, building their effect over time. Even a drip of water constantly hitting a surface over time will leave an impression.

Just as water is a life force – and a force of change – our personal impact affects the lives of others, and is a force of change. Our impact can be like a tsunami, a wave, a ripple, or a constant drip of water. Our effect can be devastating, dramatic, sweeping, or it can be gradual and subtle, and only evident over time. Just as every drop of water counts, so does everything we do. Nothing is neutral; everything counts – positive or negative –big or small. Every action either makes the world a better place, or a worse place.

Life-changing events and decisions often happen without planning or forethought, as illustrated by Rosa Park's experience. Yet, our ripple effect does not have to be dramatic to have a lasting impact. Our response to the events and circumstances of life ripples out, whether or not we are aware of it, and goes beyond those people we touch directly.

We can all relate to being on the receiving end of angry words, or disrespectful behaviours. Their impact can ruin an otherwise good day by negatively impacting our outlook and behaviour, if we permit that to happen. Similarly, when we are treated with courtesy and respect, we feel good about ourselves and pass on that positive energy. We enrich our own lives, and the lives of others when our ripple effect is positive.

I recently went on a white water rafting adventure on the Ottawa River with two friends. On the first day, we were assigned to 12-person rafts, and each raft had a guide. There were about an equal number of men and women, and I was probably the oldest person in our raft. We navigated some very turbulent rapids on the first day, including one set of rapids aptly named 'Bus Eater'. On one occasion, some of our team members were thrown out of the raft, and I was picked up and tossed back a couple of places. I certainly did not consider that I had distinguished myself in any way.

On the second day, we were in smaller, self-guided rafts, and the guides accompanied us in kayaks. We selected our group of five, connecting with a couple from our hometown of London. The London contingent was comprised of four women, and one burly policeman. One of our first tasks was to select the guide for our raft. The guide is the person who sits at the back of the raft, steers, and instructs the rest of the team what to do. The unanimous decision of our team was that 'I' would be our guide. I did not know what I had rippled out over the previous day to warrant this level of trust, yet these people were willing to trust the 'grandma' in the group, as the leader. I accepted the challenge, self-doubt raging in my brain, and thinking that my team must all be confused. As the day progressed, I found out that on occasion the guide gets to ' take one' for the team, and be tossed unmercifully into the river. However, I was not the only one to go for an unscheduled swim that day. We did successfully complete the day – success meaning surviving – and had a lot of fun along the way!

My best memory of that experience is captured in a wonderful photo showing me with a look of panic on my face, trying to keep the paddle in the water to steer while being tossed in the air with nowhere to anchor my feet. The rest of the team is calmly paddling, with smiles on their faces. The group saw something in me that allowed them to feel comfortable and confident in my leadership. My ripple effect caused that to happen.

Have you ever looked into a still pool of water and seen your image reflected back clearly? Have you ever seen the image of a majestic mountain reflected in a lake? In the same way that water reflects images, our ripple effect reflects who we are. What do you want your life to reflect?

Choosing Your Ripple Effect

Our ripple effect – or personal leadership – happens, whether or not we are aware of it, because everything we do, and say, counts. This is our personal, constant drip of water having a gradual, yet lasting, impression. The good news is that:

1) we have choice about what we ripple out, and
2) we have choice about what our lives reflect.

We can choose to live our lives by default, and unaware of our impact. We can also choose to be aware, and make conscious choices to design a life that will ripple out positively.

> **We do not accidentally end up where we end up. We create our own reality with the choices we make every day based on the foundation that we establish for ourselves.**

There are two parts to your foundation, one being your unique talents, and the other being your values.

Your Unique Talents: A common reaction is *"But I don't have a unique talent!"*, or, *"I don't know what it is."* Here are some questions for personal reflection that may help you to identify your unique talent, and there is some space for your responses below:

- What is it you enjoy?
- What are you passionate about?
- Is there one activity or thing that you do where time passes, without you losing your enthusiasm, or getting tired?
- When do you feel that you are at your best, and 'in your groove'?

_____

_____

_____

_____

_____

_____

_____

You may also find it helpful to ask trusted friends and family what they think your unique talent is, and what your strengths are. Often, other people see things in us that we do not see in ourselves. Once you have connected with your unique talent, start to consciously share that with the world. Put it out there. Your ripple effect will radiate even more effectively because you will be putting forth your best self – your optimum self.

Your Values: The second part of your foundation is your values. Most of us are able to identify a number of values that are important to us. The key is to know what four or five values are most important to you, and to use these as the main building blocks of your foundation.

> *"Don't tell me what your priorities are… Tell me what you did today, and I'll tell you what your priorities are."*
> *-Author Unknown*

Unfortunately, sometimes the things that we say are most important get shuffled to the sidelines, as 'life' takes over. We know what is important, and we may have the best-laid plans to focus on those things. Then, life happens, and all of a sudden, we are faced with several urgent matters demanding our attention. Our focus gets directed to the urgent things, and, before we know it, the important things remain undone, and frustration sets in.

How can we identify our most important values and ensure that, for the majority of the time, we are acting in alignment with them? The following exercise will help: When I am 80..........

1) How do I want to feel?
2) How do I want to be thought of?
3) What do I want my legacy to be?

_____

_____

_____

_____

_____

_____

_____

When you have answered these questions, you have identified your core values, and you have the roadmap to guide you where you want to go with your life. This is what Stephen Covey in his book, *The Seven Habits Of Highly Effective People,* refers to as '*beginning with the end in mind*'.

Some other techniques for connecting with your unique talents and your values are:

Take time to 'be': We are busy doing – activities govern our lives. Simply take 15 minutes a day for quiet time. This is only 1% of your day. You are worth it!

Meditation: Learn to meditate. Once you know how to meditate, do it, and do it consistently. Meditation connects you to your inner voice – your authenticity. Try different types of meditation until you find one that works well for you. And, give it time. It takes time to learn to quiet the mind, and allow your inner voice to emerge.

Keep a journal: Writing is a wonderful way to gain personal insight, express yourself, and work through issues. Do not worry about spelling, grammar or neatness – just get your thoughts, feelings, and insights down on paper.

Take time to be in nature: Being in nature is grounding, relaxing and healing. It is time for you to be, instead of do. We are human beings, not human doings.

Once we are aware of our unique talents and our values, we can focus on our desired outcome. Then we are able to make conscious choices, and achieve personal empowerment. This enables us to choose what our personal leadership and its impact is, and how it is going to look. Our thoughts and actions consciously and consistently reflect that. We are able to design a life that will ripple out positively.

Impactful Leadership

Some leaders are relentless and destructive. They are like a tsunami – Adolph Hitler, Saddam Hussein, and Charles Manson come to mind. Some leaders are prominent, and dynamic, creating change, and transformation, like a wave – Dr. Martin Luther King Jr., Mahatma Gandhi, and Mother Teresa. Some leaders are subtler, like a ripple, or the constant drip of water, out there day after day sharing their unique talents – Terry Fox, Rosa Parks, and Dr. Roberta Bondar.

Everyone creates a ripple effect. Everyone has a choice, whether his or her ripple effect will be positive, or negative in its impact.

> **Impactful leadership comes from living in alignment with your values and using your unique talents for the world to see.**

Likely, you will never know how far your ripple extends. You will affect someone with your leadership, and this will create a shift for that person. They will, in turn, affect someone they meet because of your influence. The third person will, in turn, pass it on, and so on, and so on.

For several years, I have been sending out a daily motivational quote by e-mail. This started with a small group of friends that I had hoped to inspire. Over the years, the group has grown in size to number in the hundreds. People pass the quotes on to friends and co-workers. Occasionally, I receive an email from someone I do not know thanking me, and telling me what a difference this daily quote means to them, as they have been receiving the quotes from a friend. I do not know how many times my daily quotes get passed on. I do not know how many lives they touch. I *do know* that my ripple is alive and well, and having a positive effect on people.

Choosing To Respond

It is clear that our response to the events and circumstances of life ripples out. This occurs whether or not we are aware of it, and it goes beyond those people who we touch directly. Sometimes, the events and circumstances of life catch us off guard. We react without thinking – and not always in the way we would have chosen to, if we had time to think about our response. One dictionary definition of *react* is to 'act in return, to act reciprocally'. When we react to a difficult situation, it is similar to a reflex action – automatic, rather than a thought-through response. We may react in kind – anger for anger – storming off, or turning to old familiar patterns of behaviour, which only serve to escalate the situation. When we do this, our ripple effect is negative.

The Four F's

When we are faced with a challenging situation, we can negatively react in one or more of four ways. These are the four F's:

Fight: The best defense is offence. Attack when attacked, which can be demonstrated verbally and physically, such as getting face-to-face, showing angry facial expressions, clenching fists, and getting steamed.

Flight: We flee the scene, and avoid confrontation or the issue. We remove ourselves, and deny that the situation exists.

Freeze: We stop communicating, withdraw, and do not respond.

Façade: We superficially pretend that everything is fine when it is not. The message sent is: 'no problems here', while our reality is different. We lie about how we truly feel to keep the peace, and avoid confrontation.

Each of these reactions creates a negative effect, and makes it difficult to resolve an issue in a constructive way. Have you ever shot back an unkind response that you regretted almost immediately? Have you ever walked away from something only to find it did not go away, and was there to face another day? Have you ever withheld your thoughts and feelings because you were afraid to share them, or to punish the other person? Have you ever said that everything was fine, when inside you were feeling angry or hurt? We have all been there, and done that, and sometimes the reaction seems automatic and unstoppable.

How can you be more consistently aware, make conscious choices, and ensure that your ripple effect will be positive, even in the most difficult circumstances? You can choose to respond, instead of react. How do you do this, rather than reacting automatically? The first step is to become aware in the moment how you react in a particular situation. As you are able to see your patterns, you will be able to catch yourself earlier in the process, until you find that you do not automatically react. Rather you can stop, and choose how-to respond. You can take time to think through your response, and make it one that will be respectful and constructive. Rather than berating yourself after the fact for a negative reaction, you will feel empowered by your ability to choose a response.

Instead of reacting with fight, flight, freeze or façade, how can you choose to respond? There are four key elements that must all be present in order to choose a respectful and constructive response.

Four Key Elements for Constructive Responding
1. *Courtesy*: Rather than reacting by being ready to fight and do battle, you can

choose to treat the other person with courtesy. This does not mean that you have to agree with them. It does mean that you can treat them with respect, and be courteous, and polite in how you deliver your response. A fighting reaction may result in another fight reaction in return, or even intimidation of the other person. Either way, the doors of communication, and resolution, are closed. When you can choose to respond in a courteous fashion, you diffuse the tension, and open the doors to communication and resolution. Your ripple effect is positive.

2. *Integrity*: Rather than fleeing from the situation, you stay and confront the issue in an effort to resolve it. Running away, and denying a situation exists, does not make it go away. It *will* resurface in the future. Facing up to the situation, even though that may be unpleasant and uncomfortable, is the only way to resolve it. It shows courage and integrity, and your ripple effect is positive.

3. *Openness*: Rather than freezing, and withholding communication, you can choose to respond, and express your thoughts and feelings. This has two benefits. It allows you to feel heard, and it lets the other person know where you stand in the situation. This opens the doors to communication, and increases the opportunities for a resolution to be found. It can seem risky to open up, and trust someone else with your thoughts and feelings. It takes courage to do this, and when you do, *your* ripple effect is positive.

4. *Honesty*: Rather than putting on a façade and pretending that everything is okay, you can respond honestly, and let the other person know that there is a problem to be addressed. When you lie by putting on a façade, you are lying to yourself as well as the other person. You are telling yourself that what you think and feel is not important enough to stand up for. It may seem easier to pretend that there is no problem, and it may be easier in the short-term. However, the situation that is not okay today will be allowed to continue, because it has been condoned through your inaction. Honouring what is important to you and expressing that honestly takes courage, and your ripple effect is positive.

While it is possible to react with one of the four F's – fight, flight, freeze or facade – it does not work to respond respectfully and constructively with only one or two of the alternate responses – courtesy, integrity, openness, and honesty. All four of these responses must be present for the ripple effect to be positive. If you choose to be courteous (stay and face the issue and communicate) yet the message you send is a façade (a lie) then you are not respectful, nor constructive. If you choose to stay and face the issue (communicate openly and honestly), yet deliver the message in a discourteous and fighting way, then you are neither respectful nor constructive. Courtesy, integrity, openness, and honesty work in conjunction with each other, not in isolation from each other.

> **When you consciously choose to respond rather than react, you achieve personal empowerment. When you choose to respond with courtesy, integrity, openness and honesty, you choose what your personal leadership and impact is going to look like, and your actions reflect that. You design a life that ripples out positively.**

The Essential Elements of a Positive Ripple Effect

The essential elements of creating a positive ripple effect are:

- respect for self,
- respect for others, and
- responsibility for all of your actions.

When you follow these three guidelines, the result is a lasting positive effect with leadership. These principles are directly linked to choosing to respond to situations in a respectful, and constructive way, with courtesy, integrity, openness, and honesty.

Respect for self means that you know who you are, and what you want your life to be about. When you have self-respect, you choose to live life by design, and not by default. Respect for self naturally ripples out to respect for others; you reflect what is important to you. When you value self-respect, and being treated with respect by others, you also know the importance of treating others with respect. You want to be treated with courtesy, integrity, openness, and honesty, and the way to invite that to happen is to set the standard, and choose to respond with courtesy, integrity, openness, and honesty. In other words, you take responsibility for all your actions. You take the lead in your own life. You do not excuse your negative behaviour by blaming others. You recognize that you have choice, and, with awareness you consciously design the life and leadership you want to have today, tomorrow, and at age 80. You begin with the end in mind, by acting in alignment with your values and unique talents every day.

Everything Counts

Can conscious personal leadership and having positive ripple effect be this simple and straightforward? Remembering the following will help:

Everything counts – Positive or negative it ripples out.
Act in alignment with your values, and share your unique talents.
Choose to respond with courtesy, integrity, openness, and honesty.
Respect for self, respect for others, and responsibility for all your actions.

Yes! It is that simple and straightforward. Don't the realities of life get in the way and make this difficult? Yes, sometimes they do. The question really becomes, 'Who is in control'? Is it the situations, and circumstances of life, or are we in charge? Do we live by default or by design? It is up to each of us.

> *One day, a man was walking along the beach when he noticed a figure in the distance. As he got closer, he realized the figure was that of a boy picking something up, and gently throwing it into the ocean. Approaching the boy he asked, "What are you doing?" The youth replied, "Throwing a starfish into the ocean. The sun is up and the tide is going out. If I don't throw them back they'll die."*
> *"Son", the man said, "Don't you realize there are miles and miles of beach, and hundreds of starfish? You can't possibly make a difference!" After listening politely, the boy bent down, picked up another starfish, and threw it into the surf. Then, smiling at the man, he said, "I made a difference to that one".*
> — Brian Biro, 'Beyond Success:
> The Fifteen Secrets of a Winning Life'

We each make a difference, whether the impact is like a tsunami, a wave, a ripple, or a drip of water. When we make conscious choices to do the best we can, where we are, with what we have, our ripple effect is positive, and we make the world a better place. How do you choose to design your life? How will your personal leadership impact?

If you can't make waves, make ripples.

Biography for Janet Christensen

Business Name: Unlimiting Potential
Business Address: P.O. Box 25572
395 Wellington Rd. S.,
London, Ontario N6C 6B3
Telephone: (519) 434-5397
Fax: (519) 434-8344
Email: janet.christensen@sympatico.ca
Web Address: www.janetchristensen.com

Canadian Association of Professional Speakers Chapter:
Southwestern Ontario, Local Member

About Janet:

Janet Christensen's passion is to empower people to live their full potential. Through her company, Unlimiting Potential, she inspires personal development as a coach, facilitator and speaker. Her seminar and keynote topics include: 'If You Can't Make Waves, Make Ripples', 'The Courage To Be Who You Are', and 'Fear – Friend Or Foe?' Janet's presentations are described as inspiring, enlightening, and impacting. Her expertise in personal development makes her a valued choice, whether it's one-on-one as a coach, or as a speaker or facilitator for a group or a conference. Some of the organizations that have benefited from Janet's expertise and leadership include Lifestream Canada, London & St. Thomas Real Estate Board, Masala Management Network, Canadian Diabetes Association, and Ontario March of Dimes.

Janet has a B.A. from the University of Western Ontario, is completing the Associate Certified Coach Program with the International Coaching Academy, is a member of Coachville, and a licensed Realtor. Janet has Reiki Third Degree. She is a two-time recipient of the President's Circle Club Award from REALTY WORLD Corporation for Manager of the Year (Ontario), 1994 and 1995. Her varied professional background includes management, training and facilitation, sales, personnel, and customer service.

Favourite Quote:

> *"Be the change you want to see in the world."*
> *- Mahatma Gandhi*

Storying Our Lives …
Using Story in the
21st Century and Beyond

By: Jean Ryan
Jean Ryan & Associates

Once upon a time…

Wait! Don't go away! That was just a test. How did you react to that opening line? I suspect most people had an immediate response of one sort or another. Perhaps you wondered what sort of a childish article this was going to be, or you may have been eager for a good story. That line is the phrase that began the fairy tales of our youth, stories we loved to hear over and over again. So, what does that have to do with us as adults, and why would you be interested, anyway? In this chapter, you'll get a brief look at oral tradition, a peek at what has been called the Storytelling Revival, a birds-eye view of the ever-expanding arenas where story is in use today, and a glimpse at how to use storytelling in your own life. But let's start at the beginning.

Stories from Yesteryear

Before there were stories, there were words. Every society that has ever existed used words. There may have been gestures and grunts to begin with, but as the numbers of people grew, sounds became connected with objects. Certain sounds were repeated and when I realized that every time you pointed to the tree you made that sound, I tried making the sound and pointing to the tree. Eureka…verbal language!

Our ancestors survived through story. Stories were used to tell where the game was, where the best water holes were, where the best patch of wild yams had been found. Stories were told of great hunts and heroic deeds. While we do not have complete records of those stories, perhaps you have been lucky enough to travel to see the paintings in the Chauvet caves in France. Closer to home, Ontario has the largest concentration of aboriginal rock carvings in North America. They can be found in the Petroglyph Park in the Peterborough area, where over 900 petroglyphs of birds, snakes, turtles, and humans were carved into the white marble face of rocks over 1,200 years ago. It is clear that even our pre-historic ancestors felt the need to get their ideas across, and have them passed on from one to the other, and left behind for those yet to come.

As people began to form societies, they shared their stories and began to identify with others in their groups. He or she of the valiant deeds was one of us, not 'Them'. Stories evolved as tools for shaping the identity of the group, for passing on values and customs, for sharing good news and bad.

As societies became more complex, trade with other groups began, and there was a new problem to tackle. Those 'Others' did not use the same sounds we did, so we found ways to get the point across – gestures and drawings in the dirt were no doubt the first steps. Trade languages evolved – 'lingua franca', as it came to be known in the Mediterranean – which allowed traders and merchants from different cultures to communicate. Given the new common languages, it is easy to imagine early traders sitting around campfires sharing stories – learning that they had things in common – and marvelling at their differences.

Writing and Books

As written language evolved, the fluidity of the spoken word was lost. Rules were formulated, and language became a tool of the group in power. The people with positions of authority in the dominant culture were the ones who made up the rules of grammar and usage. In most cases these were religious leaders, lawgivers, and doctors. The rules became more complex, and certain forms of language became the markers of power. Many scholars believe that the rules of language often were created with the intent of mystifying and confusing the working people and the poor people who spoke differently, and rarely read. With the advent of the printing press, books became more available. Remember that the representatives of the group in power wrote the books. The type of language used and the values expressed reflected *that* group's thinking.

That's nice, you say, but what does this have to do with stories? Anyone who grew up in the European tradition knows of, or at least has heard of, the Brothers Grimm. I, for one, had a romanticized view of them traipsing across the countryside, collecting the stories, and making them available to all. It seems, however, that even the Brothers Grimm had an agenda. They gathered the tales, and altered them to suit their own beliefs – to reflect their ideas of how the world should operate. So, the tales we have taken as a reflection of a particular place and time are, in fact, the revisionist tales of two men with a particular world view.

But, what about the little people? Oral tradition had continued on, and the stories reflected the thoughts and feelings of those who were telling and those who were listening. Many times, the tellers would change the stories to include local place names or even bits of local news. The stories were meant for these particular people on this particular day.

The Storytelling Revival

In the 1970s, in both the United States and Canada, the seeds of a movement which has been called the Storytelling Revival started to sprout. There are those who say that it was part of the renewed interest in folk music, and the 'return to the land' groups. Whatever the reason, storytelling groups sprang up. In 1972, what has become the largest and most well-known association of its kind in the U.S. was begun in Jonesboro, Tennessee. That group is now known as the National Storytelling Network, and Jonesboro hosts a huge storytelling event every October. In Canada, Toronto's *1001 Nights* has offered a place for tellers and listeners to get together every Friday night since 1978. There are guilds and groups, gatherings and festivals all over North America and abroad. And the stories are not just for children or special events; they have crept into all aspects of our society. How are we using this magic today? Read on.

Stories Today

Stories are being used in virtually every aspect of today's society. The surprising thing is that most people are unaware of it. Let's take a look at some of the uses of story in the world around us.

"I see my whole life wrapped in stories – or rather, my lives, as son, brother, husband, father, reader, writer, editor, friend: in each of these storytelling plays a large role."
- Robert Fulford, journalist

Families

Most of us seem to be living hectic lives, driven by schedules. What talk there is revolves around what things are on the go – whether Susie's soccer tournament is more important that Billy's Tae Kwan Do exhibition on the other side of town. Conversation? No such animal. But what if part of the problem was that families don't know how to talk to each other? What if a tiny part of every day was spent actually relating to each other? What if there was less go-go-go and a little more 'be'. Sharing stories can provide that sense of 'being'.

Many surveys have shown that children who are told stories from very early on are more apt to be better readers and have broader vocabularies. They also learn active listening skills. Recent studies have indicated that children are losing their ability to visually imagine, presumably because our culture has provided them with TV, video, and movies. Stories offer an opportunity to create a visual world of their own design – colourful, changeable, magical.

The use of stories to stimulate communication between generations is increasing by leaps and bounds. Elders are learning to tell their own stories, and finding that they are of interest to others – family members and beyond. Children are discovering that 'old people' have some awesome experiences to share. When the generations share stories, connections are established, self-esteem is fostered, and family histories are often preserved.

> *"There is no such thing as a boring life story."*
> *- Carol Shields, Pulitzer Prize winning author*

Schools

There is a great concern today about bullying, especially in schools and on the playgrounds. There are storytellers who have put together shows focused on bullying and the harm it can do. One teller I know talks about a young girl coming up to her after a performance, and tearfully blurting out that she recognized herself in the character of the bully. She said she never wanted to behave that way again.

There are many storytellers who focus on telling stories in schools. Some provide entertainment; many specialize in programmes tailored to the curriculum. They can bring history and literature alive for the children in a way that textbooks cannot. Stories will supply a way to connect with children who have a variety of learning styles.

> *Tell me a fact and I'll learn.*
> *Tell me a truth and I'll believe.*
> *But tell me a story and it will live in my heart forever.*
> *- Proverb*

Community Building

Salman Rushdie, the acclaimed author, has referred to the last 200 years or so as the 'Migration Period'. People left their towns and villages, moved across national borders, and even across continents. They left their communities, and started anew. While those moves have had some wonderful consequences, many people feel somehow disconnected from the place where they live. In large urban areas especially, it is common for us not to know our neighbours, or the name of the shopkeepers we see every week. We hear about having pride in our community, but somehow, that is often just a place where our home is, not the people who are around us. Stories can be used to develop a sense of belonging, and to share values. They can also help us to reconnect with our forbearers and the cultures they knew, and the culture that forms part of who we are today.

> *A neighbourhood in a large metropolitan city was having a festival, and one enlightened soul approached members of a particular ethnic group and asked if they would participate. She asked if they would tell their stories – stories from their culture of origin, stories about how they came to Canada, and what it was like for them after they arrived. There was some trepidation, but the new people felt obliged to take part. They got together to decide what to say and how to go about it, all the time wondering if anyone would care. The result was that the newcomers rediscovered some of their own traditions. The wider community learned about a beautiful culture that they had not been aware of – and it was a part of their own community! Neighbours began to extend smiles, and then hands, because a barrier had been removed. 'They' were no longer people to be viewed with suspicion or fear. 'They' were people just like 'Us' – perhaps a bit different in diet or appearance, but 'They', too, had stories filled with heartache and joy.*

Reg Davidson is an internationally renowned Haida artist – mask maker, carver, jewellery maker, singer and dancer. In interviews, he has spoken about his start as a craftsman, and how his art changed and developed after he had re-connected with stories from his grandmother. Learning the stories, his understanding of the language grew. The Haida language contained phrases and references that led him to find out more about the culture. The cultural journey took him to dancing and singing, and he is one of the founders of the Rainbow Creek Dancers who are dedicated to performing Haida songs and dances. The words in those stories and the references to what people did, and felt, and saw, that took him to places he had not been aware of in his youth.

'Tapestry: An Arab-Jewish Storytelling Dialogue' is a storytelling performance which grew from the concerns of B.J. Abraham and Audrey Galex, two tellers who were overwhelmed by feelings of helplessness and concern about the escalating violent conflict in the Middle East. They began to meet and share stories of their childhood – of how each of them grew up 'different', one as a Lebanese girl and the other immersed in her Jewish heritage. They discovered that, as adults, each had traveled to the Middle East and found those trips life-altering. So began a series of presentations and performances based on their shared experiences, folklore and peace tales. Their own understanding and compassion grew as did that of their audiences.

Healing

> *"Stories that are filled with positive, healing images can create a physiological state that biochemists would associate with health, relaxation, and emotional well-being."*
> *- Richard Stone, from The Healing Art of Storytelling*

Stories have long been felt to have healing qualities. Today they are used in many health related areas: in counseling, palliative care, with cancer survivors, the bereaved, with victims of abuse, and recovering addicts. Stories are being used for personal growth and in conjunction with both traditional and alternative therapies. They are used to help children and adults who were orphaned or adopted get a sense of who they are. They are helping children in areas struck by disaster to hang on to hope for the future and faith in humanity despite the devastation they have witnessed.

Clarissa Pinkola Estes, most widely know as the author of *Women Who Run With the Wolves*, is an author, poet, Jungian analyst, and most importantly is a 'cantadora'. A 'cantadora', in the Latina tradition, is the keeper of the old stories – she is given a position of great responsibility and trust. Due to her unique blend of talent and education, Dr. Estes was appointed from 1999-2002 as 'Artist-in-Residence' at Columbine High School, the site of the attack on students by fellow students. Her use of poetry and story was aimed at assisting the students to acknowledge what had happened, to mourn their lost friends, and to move forward in their own lives.

Here is another example of the power of storytelling for healing:

> *The hospital asked for a storyteller to provide entertainment at a Patient Appreciation luncheon on Valentine's Day. The average age of the group was 75 years, and many were in very poor health. At the end of the performance, the teller noticed one man was crying – not small trickles of tears, but a steady stream accompanied by ragged breath and heaving shudders. Disturbed by the thought that her stories had caused the man pain, she later learned that previously this man had not opened up to anyone. He had sat alone and aloof, not impolite, but very private. The stories had touched him in a way nothing else was able to, allowing him to finally share his sorrows and his joys.*

Business

Both large and small organizations have to make hard decisions about their own survival. They claim it is difficult to find good employees. The employees feel that they are nothing more than furniture – tossed aside when the next CEO arrives with this year's views on downsizing or de-centralizing.

What if the corporate culture was explored, and the stories within brought to light? What if the people behind the front lines were made known to each other through the use of story? What if new employees were recruited in part based on their clear understanding of the values held by the company, the men and women who worked there every day. Those values and hopes and dreams can be contained in a story…in their stories. Many organizations have begun to discover that using the power of storytelling, in addition to their analytical processes, is yielding unexpected results. Is it possible, then, that there might be loyalty, long-term relationships, and less absenteeism? There are storytellers currently working with exactly these issues, using their skills to assist both employers and employees to cope and move ahead.

> *"I've never seen a great military, political or corporate leader who was not a great storyteller. Telling stories is a core competency in business, although it's one that we don't pay enough attention to."*
> *- Brian Ferren, The Disney Corporation*

Entertainment (last but certainly not least!)

This is all very nice, you say, but people won't sit still for stories. Well, that is not really true. A small storytelling guild had offered a free story concert on a Sunday afternoon. It turned out to be the first really sunny, warm Sunday of that spring, and the entire audience was comprised of one mother and three little girls. The girls were around eight or nine, and the tellers thought it would all be over in about a half an hour. Four tellers ended up telling stories non-stop for an hour and a half! The girls did not want a break, and sat quietly, still and wide-eyed for all that time.

Telling Stories – Some Basics

So… now that you know the value and some of the uses of story, how do you do it? The first thing is to understand what a story is. In its simplest form, it is a recounting of events – real or imagined. The ancient Celts referred to storytelling as painting a picture with words. The best news is there is no wrong way. There is only one rule – DON'T READ IT! Here are some ideas to help you get started.

Look: Do not look for a 'thing'– just look! Most of us are in such a hurry to run from place to place, we don't notice the world around us. Make the time to really look. It will bring you surprising results – a new idea that solves a problem, or makes you smile.

Another aspect of looking is changing perspective. Just for fun, step into the space ahead of where you are right now – ahead and to the right or left. Now, turn and look back. Make believe that you are a stranger, seeing 'you' for the first time. What do you see? Watch how 'you' interact with others – how 'you' moves. Seeing a story from another vantage point will often reveal some wondrous detail that might have been overlooked if you had not changed your sight line.

Sensory Input: Smell is the sense most strongly tied with memory. So, what can you add to you story in the way of smell? What about the way the sun feels on your skin or the texture of a piece of cloth? How about the background noises – is a bird singing? frozen grass crunching? All those things add depth and interest to a story.

Listen: The annual Toronto Festival of Storytelling has a catch phrase: 'Listen Up'. What we seem to do most is 'listen down'. We tune out…so much so that often we do not hear what is going on around us. Pay attention, not only to what is being said but how it is said. Notice the rhythm of language. Be alert for phrases and bits of conversation that you can use in your own stories. Listen to the silences, the pauses, the words unspoken.

Research: Begin in the children's section of your local library. Look for fairy tales or folklore, stories you liked. Look for books of local history or ghost stories. Start with something small – a short piece well told will be an easier place to start than a Greek epic. Above all, whether you try traditional stories or personal stories, make sure you really like the material. If you don't like it, chances are you will not tell it well, and that means no one else will like it either.

Voice: Voice is one of your most powerful tools. Use it well. Put energy in your voice – speed it up to show that the action is moving faster, soften it to show tenderness or compassion. Make sure you can be heard without shouting, and beware of 'swallowing' words – the listener really wants to hear what you have to say.

Learn: How often do you refer to your day-timer, hand-held computer, and check your diary? How could you possibly learn a story when you can't remember what day it is? Some tellers learn a story word for word. The danger with memorizing is that if you forget a word, or lose your place, you are sunk. Others 'learn' the story by reading it over and over. What if you forget a line? Don't worry about it. Think the story through, use notes, make mental pictures, but most of all connect with it – use your imagination and allow yourself some room for expansion or reduction. It's your story – take ownership!

You need to know where you are going before you begin. I have often had an end in mind, and no idea of how I was going there. The story just seems to take me along. If you have stopped, looked, listened – and used your heart rather than your head – the story will speak to you too. Try to be IN the story when you tell it, as if you were another character – an observer if you will. Feel the cold wind across the Siberian plane, smell the salt air on the sea coast of Scotland, taste the wine in the French vineyard.

Practise: Make sure you practise out loud, without an audience first. Try saying the story in a cemetery – you have peace and quiet, and the residents are not likely to complain. Others pace around the room, or practise in the car. Yes, other drivers look at you funny, but so what – you have just given them a story to tell!

Speak!: At home, you can begin with telling what happened during the day – not only the events, but also how you felt about them. Start with the youngest person first. They are eager to share. Give them some encouragement, support them in their trials, and offer positive feedback. If you don't have children, try telling a story to your friends – nothing formal, just a recounting, but without the usual stock phrases of complaint. Try stepping back, and creating a small story – even only a minute long – which incorporates what you saw, felt, and did. Make it a game to lessen the pressure, and see who can come up with the most engaging story.

At work, start by inquiring. Ask a co-worker a question the next time you are at the water-cooler, or the coffee pot. The trick is to ask open-ended questions, that is questions that cannot be answered by 'yes', or 'no', or a single word. WARNING: this may actually lead to a conversation, or enrich your workday!

And then…

The basic themes of stories remain, but details change, and flow, and adapt. The spoken word changes even as it passes from the brain, over the teeth, and out through the mouth. It re-forms itself with bits of the environment – the weather, the mood of the group, the adventures of the teller on the way to the event. The tale will never be exactly the same twice. And, that is a good thing.

I believe in the strength of stories
to establish connections where none had existed before,
the magic of metaphor
to bring clarity where there had been confusion, and
the immensity of imagination to provide illumination and iridescence
to the all of worlds we are fortunate enough to encounter.

So, take the plunge! Tell the story you remember loving as a child. Tell the story of what happened when you lost your first tooth, or did something you never thought you could. Just start telling, and you will find that helpers abound – in story – and in real life, too.

Who knows? You may just live … happily ever after!

Resources

Want more information about storytellers, groups or gatherings in your area? In Canada the national organization is the Storytellers of Canada/Conteurs du Canada. Their website at: www.sc-cc.com, includes links to tellers and happenings across the country. In Ontario, The Storytellers School of Toronto is a rich source of information about province wide events and includes a directory of members. The School also has a website: www.storytelling.org. In the United States, the National Storytelling Network can be contacted through their site www.storynet.org.

Biography for Jean Ryan

Business Name:	Jean Ryan & Associates
Address:	2066 Lakeshore Road West, Oakville, Ontario L6L 1G7
Telephone:	(905) 847-3976
Fax:	(905) 847-9349
Email:	jf.ryan@sympatico.ca
Web Address:	coming in 2003

Canadian Association of Professional Speakers Chapter:
Hamilton, Associate member

About Jean:

Jean Ryan, often called the 'Word Weaver', is a professional storyteller and speaker, writer, facilitator, coach and consultant. Her storytelling expertise adds a unique twist to her speaking ability. In her keynote and workshop presentations, she incorporates both traditional and original stories that are customized for the audience.

She has delighted and captivated community and business groups with such presentations as *'Brāno...Plumbing the Depths of the Communication Pipeline'*, and 'Give Yourself Some L-Attitude'. She has also developed a workshop on *'Storytelling 101: the Basics of Telling a Story'*, of interest to speakers, teachers, trainers, and facilitators wanting to enhance their presentations.

Jean has more than 25 years in the financial services sector, where she has earned designations as a Fellow Chartered Insurance Professional. She has an Honours B.A. as a specialist in Social Cultural Anthropology, and holds certificates in Teaching and Training Adults, Teaching English as a Second Language, and as a Master Trainer. She is currently enrolled in the Certificate of Writing program at McMaster University.

Along with CAPS, her memberships include the Storytellers of Canada, the National Storytellers Network (US), the Storytellers School of Toronto, the Burlington Storytellers Guild, the Ontario Society for Training and Development and the Canadian Association of NLP.

Influencing With Wisdom

By: Valerie Cade Lee CSP
Performance Curve International

How to confidently say what you want –
and not at the expense of yourself or others.

Have you ever had the experience of not saying what you wanted to say? You said something totally different just for acceptance, yet underneath, you wanted something else? Perhaps you didn't say anything at all. Maybe you were even secretly angry with the other person because they didn't read your mind? Have you ever had the experience of saying something you felt you had the right to say, yet, what you said wasn't accepted? In fact, you became more upset because of the rejection from having said it?

Have you noticed there are people in this world that seem to have the ability to influence others' thinking and decisions in a win/win way? The key is influencing with wisdom. How can we communicate our own needs while honouring the needs of another? Having this skill set mastered can help you gain credibility, respect, and loyalty for years to come. There are some steps that you can learn through this chapter. Are you ready?

> *Influencing with wisdom is the key to enabling win/win situations.*

Why Do We Do What We Do?

Imagine you've been dating your university sweetheart for three years. You are both broke, but you receive a note to meet at a fancy restaurant on Friday night. Could it be time for 'the question'? Sure enough, after dinner, your honey gets down on one knee and asks: *"Will you marry me?"* .... *"...ah, yes."*

And for 120 days thereafter, you have this gut-wrenching feeling, because what you really wanted to say was "No!" Have you ever said 'yes' when you wanted to say 'no'? For 120 days, *I* had this gut-wrenching feeling. The stress, and indecision of saying 'yes' when I wanted to say 'no' got so bad, that at age 22, I developed an ulcer, had lost hair off my head, and I was hospitalized for a day to replace my bodily fluids!

Twenty-two days before the marriage was to occur, I drove over to my then-fiancé's house, expecting one of those long talks. He was a wonderful man. In fact, many of my friends and family had commented the same. They wanted me to get married. I knocked on the door. It took only one minute: *"I'm not able to marry you."* Many people couldn't understand why I would do such a thing. Honestly, it wasn't until five years after the fact that I realized I had the right to have what I wanted, too! Yes, it was hard and, ironically, many years later, I realized that speaking my truth then enhanced my well being today. It was the best decision. I'll ask you. *Do you believe that speaking your truth is in your best interest, and if not, why not?*

The Courage to Speak Your Truth

Could it be that we may sometimes put stress on ourselves from not speaking our truth? The question is: Why would we not speak our truth in a case like this? These may be some of the reasons:

1. *Believing we don't have the right to have needs.* This is especially true if they are different from someone else's. We believe their needs are more important to ours.

2. *Believing that we don't have the right to express our needs.* This occurs because of fears of rejection, of not being accepted, not being liked, or not being included. Both fear of expressing our needs (fear of rejection), and the feeling that we don't have the right to have the needs are based on feelings of low self worth. These come from deep, unconscious beliefs such as: 'Nice people don't make waves.' 'If it's going to hurt them, I don't have the right to speak my truth and 'I must back down to meet their needs and not my own', and, 'They might get angry.'

Ask yourself: *'If I speak my truth in a win/win way, what's the worst thing that could happen?'* Often, the reality isn't as bad as we imagine. Consider the following, and check off the ones that you find yourself thinking:

- ❑ They will not like me.
- ❑ They will be mad at me.
- ❑ They will no longer include me.
- ❑ They will not accept me.
- ❑ They may be upset with the situation, but not with me.
- ❑ They may be angry, and this is ok.
- ❑ They may feel hurt, and this is ok.

Know ultimately, that:

- The sun will still rise tomorrow…!
- They may seek to understand me.
- They will respect me for speaking my truth, but the respect might not happen right away, because they are either hurt, angry, or they are blaming me for their feelings. Know that this is ok.

When we hold back saying what we want to say, or hold back sharing our truth – not out of privacy – but out of fear, this results in behaviour that is *passive*. Behaviour that is passive is acting at the expense of ourselves. We give into others' needs, and deny our own.

Point to Ponder: Do I feel worthy enough to feel like I can speak my truth? Do I feel confident enough to speak my truth?

> *Have you ever been in a situation like this? You're in a seminar, and the answers you came for are not being addressed. You promptly put up your hand and say, "Can we get this seminar moving, and get onto the real issues?" After everyone hears your statement, the tension mounts in the room, and there is a feeling of discomfort. Yes, your question is answered, and no, you don't feel as connected to the others as you were before.*

Question: Is this a win/win statement? Clearly, this statement is one of judgment and blame. It is behaviour that is aggressive. The real question is: 'How can we voice our truth so that it is not at the expense of others?'

What causes behaviour that is aggressive? There are several sources. It grows out of anger and frustration, which may come from a sense of powerlessness or loss of control. In some cases, it is a learned behaviour, as the only role model a person has seen for self-expression has been someone with behavioural aggression. How would this person know any differently? Another situation occurs where someone has not said their thoughts or truth for a long time, and they display overkill, and simply want to make the point, but are received as being aggressive.

In other cases, we know the difference, and we've chosen the behaviour that is aggressive because we feel we can get our results that way. Thoughts go through our mind such as: *'I'm ok, you're not!' 'If they did it just the way I would do it, then we wouldn't have this problem.'* Our beliefs are often ones that tell us the other person 'owes us something', thereby, putting the other person on a lower playing field than ourselves. We may appear as judgmental and blaming as a result of these beliefs.

Point to Ponder: What eventual outcome do you want as a result of speaking your truth? Is it the need to control the situation, or the need for win/win connection?

Here is another situation. Sexually, you imply to your partner, *"Yes, this is good"*. Yet, you have thoughts of, *"Why does it have to be this way?" "I wish that..."* – perhaps for years! You are frustrated, yet you don't say anything. You are also angry at this situation, and you might even 'get back' at your partner by not making a special effort like you used to, or you give them the silent treatment sometimes because your needs are not met in this other area. It is the 'getting back at' that is aggressive, and the not saying anything in the first place is passive. This is known as *passive-aggressive* behaviour. Eventually, the other person ends up feeling uncomfortable and distanced, and they do not even know why. You experience a lack of inner congruency, as your feelings and actions do not match.

Point to Ponder: If your needs are not being met, who's responsibility is it to try and meet those needs (in a win/win way of course)? Assertive communication is saying what you want, not at the expense of yourself or others. It is said in such a way that honours you, and it is not offensive, rude, nor judgmental to the other person. The easiest way to check to see if we are displaying behavior that is assertive is to be aware of our thoughts when we are conversing with others. Proactive thoughts are:

- 'I'm a worthy person, and so are you.'
- 'I have rights to my opinions and thoughts, and so do you.'
- 'Conflicts – or raising issues of possible discomfort – are opportunities to grow, and shouldn't be avoided, especially if avoiding them will cause further tension or harm.'

Point to Ponder: Do you believe you have the right and the ability to express your needs without being at the expense of yourself or others? If others do not agree with or accept what you say or, perhaps, how you said it, are you open to feedback from them for a win/win connection?

Should We Always Speak Our Truth?
Here is an example from many years ago:

> *There was a truck that parked on a narrow street, right in front of a woman's parking spot, to drop off some items to a business nearby. She immediately called the police to have the truck removed. In fact, when someone asked her whom she was calling, she said, "Security, he's blocking my parking spot!" When she told me of this story, I asked if she needed to get out of her parking spot at that time, and she said "No". It was the principle and that was her spot!*

My question: Is this the fight to pick? What was the need to speak her truth here? Was this more about control, as opposed to win/win connection?

You will encounter many times where you will feel like saying something right away, yet you will have to evaluate if saying something right away – or even saying it at all – is the best option. For example, say you have a very good rapport and a lot of goodwill built up with a fellow committee member. In fact, she has helped you out in your career quite a bit. There is something about this person you don't necessarily warm up to. They tend to talk a lot, but only at times. When they do, you get a little bit frustrated. One day, you're on the phone, and your colleague cuts you off in conversation. You immediately say, *"I considered you cutting me off rude, and I wasn't finished my sentence."*

Two issues: could it be possible you are looking for a way to 'put them in their place' since you listen to them 'go on' sometimes? Could it be that this person didn't even realize they had cut you off? Do you think their intent was for win/lose? Would this be the time and place to speak up?

Point to Ponder: As you find yourself being more confident with who you are, you will feel less of a need to be 'understood', and you will feel less of a need to speak up every time. You will be less concerned with asserting your boundaries, and more concerned with the overall long-term effectiveness of what you say, and how it affects the well-being of others. Maybe you don't agree? What do you think of this story?: While eating lunch outside with my business associate, Aime, a bee was buzzing by. I was swatting at the bee to go away and to no avail. It was also interrupting our conversation when Aime said to me, *"Why are you swatting at the bee? Are you going to let a bee control you? What would happen if you let it go?"* Thanks, Aime. To this day, I do not swat bees. What else can we let go?

> **When we let go, we release the need to control, and we become attractive to others. Now, we are in a position to influence with wisdom.**

Influencing Others with Wisdom

I know that 'on paper', it seems we have a choice in everything we do. It's when we get into the heat of the moment that we may see differently. In any given situation, we have three choices:

1) We can change the situation, such as using some of the proactive choices that we have already discussed. The goal is not to try and change the other person directly, but perhaps they will change by you having changed your behaviour first.

2) Another choice is to leave the situation. The key is to leave because we have either tried everything, or the situation is no longer profitable to be engaged in. This is as opposed to leaving because of fear of feeling uncomfortable, as we are not dealing with the situation directly, when there would be long-term benefits to doing so. Don't leave without the lesson!

3) Lastly, our choice is to accept the situation. Accepting is different than tolerating. Accepting means letting go. As we mature, we are able to let go of more.

Not Saying Anything... Still Influential?

Most people work at trying to figure out what to 'say' so they can be influential. They feel they have to say something. Many times, we can be influential by not saying anything at all, and coming to a place of acceptance. However, for those times when we feel we must say something, or try and shape the matter differently, we look at what our parents taught us: *It's not what you say; it's how you say it.* I believe that if we have accepting beliefs of others around us in a given situation, as opposed to a belief of 'they owe me', or a belief of 'I'll show them', then whatever we say, most times will be in harmony and not offend. We take the risk away that many of us wonder about; *'Will I hurt them when I say this?'* Basically, if we have an attitude of care and acceptance to start with, this will be communicated in the message to the other person even though we may have to deliver a difficult message.

Point to Ponder: Is there ever a reason to deliver a message to another person if there first isn't an attitude of care and acceptance?

What If We Don't Feel an Attitude of Care and Acceptance?

Here's where exercising maturity helps. You have a choice. Which one will you choose? Will you speak up and think, 'So what?', like my friend with the truck in the driveway, and risk alienating others? Or will you pull back for a while, and let your negative emotions simmer until you can approach the other person in a win/win way? Maybe you don't even approach them at all because you realize this is not a fight to pick. This is similar to writing a scathing reply to an email. You know better than to press SEND, so you save it, thinking you will later send a modified version. The next day you re-read and delete. It is no longer a fight to pick…at least, not in this way. Taking time out is a mature way to get centered, and save possible damage to your relationships and ultimately, your character.

Giving Necessary Feedback

Gently emphasize your case, so everyone can save face: Do you believe you should speak up if 'the rules are being broken', or there is a misunderstanding, even if it means that it may be difficult to do so? Do you generally give the feedback? If you could do it without it being at the expense of yourself or others, would you do it? Of course! Here are some tips you can use that honour this principle:

Benefit of the Doubt: After 25 'Thank-you for Not Smoking' signs were posted in the office, 'Phil' (not his real name) came in smoking. I was all set to get mad, but then, remembered the phrase above: gently *emphasize my case so everyone can save face*. I changed my approach. I remembered Phil has rights and needs, and so do I. He is a human being, too, and there is no need for World War Three tactics.

"*Hey Phil, I'm curious, you may not be aware, but there is No Smoking here*". *To which he replied, "Oh, I didn't know that."* Now, I knew that he knew and he knew that I knew he knew, but 'the benefit of the doubt' and being curious allowed him to save face. Next time when I saw Phil, there wasn't that uncomfortable feeling of having being reprimanded, and he wasn't smoking, either.

Self-Disclosure: When I was giving feedback to an employee in my office about being late, I realized that, if I called them on the fact, that they might make excuses and be very defensive. Self-disclosure works well here because you allow the other person to realize that other people make mistakes too, as in a phrase like, "I used to be late, too. I understand. There's always so much to do." It doesn't make an excuse for being late, it merely addresses the fact that many people are late, and opens the door to possible behaviour change.

Opinions and Facts: So, you feel you have to say something to your friend. When you are in public with others, your friend means well, but her jokes put you down. It's bothering you, and you feel it would be for the good of your friendship.

In this case, it is your opinions, and how you feel, as opposed to facts that you will reference. Speaking from your own reference is less defensive, because they are your references, and no one can take them away. You might say: *"Susan, I'm curious about something. When we were at the party on Saturday night and you said that joke about how I can't cook very well, I felt embarrassed."* Susan may respond by saying, *"Oh I didn't mean anything by it."* Or, she may be silent, or she may say *"Sorry!"* You want to make sure she understands, so she doesn't do it again, so you re-state how you felt: *"Actually I really did feel embarrassed."*

Re-stating firms your position, and makes it a stronger point. Many have called this the 'Broken Record Technique'. Now, you can add something stronger if need be: *"It would be good to leave me out of the joke, perhaps." "Can we do this, Yes or No?"* If she says *"Sure"*, then you have an agreement. If she says *"No"*, then do what little kids do, and ask "Why?" Remember, if she refuses to change her behaviour, then your next option is to really share how it makes you feel, while coming from a belief of caring and concern for both of you. Next, know that it says more about her than you, and start the process of letting go of the need for a certain outcome (such as her changing), and accept the situation if you can. You may not like it, but you can learn to accept it.

Letting Go of the Need to Control: An Issue of Self Worth: Here's another situation. I had a colleague who called me 'Kiddo'! When I heard this, I felt like a child, and thought, 'Does he think I'm a child'? I was concerned about what he thought, and even doubted my abilities in business and speaking compared to him! For years I envisioned 'having a chat some day', and I would tell him. Over the years, I weighed out telling him, and the affects this would produce, versus not telling him, and seeing some other way out of this. Finally, we were in a situation where we were talking for an extended period of time. I thought, 'This is it'! But after few hours, I realized I didn't need to say it. This was my lesson in self-acceptance, not in changing someone else. It felt good to let it go! What a lesson. Maybe someday, I'll tell him the whole story! What caused the change? I realized my own self worth, and I was less concerned with how someone else viewed me in these terms.

Getting a Clear Agreement After Acceptance From Your Feedback: Let's say you give some feedback to a co-worker about being late for meetings. They say they will now be on time. Here's what you do to secure the agreement: *'Just so I'm clear, our agreement is we will be on time and if we can't make it, we'll call no later than one hour before to see if we can re-schedule.'* By bringing this agreement to closure by restating it, the other person has another chance to hear it, and begins to realize you mean business. This helps with accountability, as there is now a clear agreement to start with to hold the accountability in place,.

Ensuring Accountability Takes Place: Have you ever wanted to give some feedback, perhaps on a broken agreement, but you felt you were not clear on the agreement, or it was vague, so you felt less confident in voicing your needs? As mentioned above, the phrase, saying, *'Just so I'm clear, our agreement is…'* sets up the awareness of a mutual agreement.

Some ways to secure the follow through might be to send an email after saying, *'Looking forward to our meeting at 1pm'.* If there is a broken agreement, again, give them the benefit of the doubt and state, *'I thought our agreement was'.* This allows the other person to come clean, and it preserves their dignity as well. And, it could be that *you* are wrong in your timing and wouldn't that be embarrassing!

Lastly, if you experience a chronically repeated broken agreement, ask: *'What will we do if we break this agreement?'* Here's an example:

> *I had a client I was coaching, and when we 'd meet, he wouldn't have his 'homework' done. I asked him, "Do you want to be held accountable?" He said, "Oh yes!" I said "How badly?" He replied, "Badly!". So, I asked him to make me out a cheque for $5,000. I said "If you have these four items done for next time, then I'll give you your cheque back. If you don't, I'll be going shopping." He then asked if he could do only three items, and he'd let me keep*

the cheque. We did this all summer. He was realistic, and accountable, and I never did go shopping.

Managing Behaviour that is Aggressive: Remember that communicative behaviour that appears aggressive is a result of feeling a need to control. What can we do with another person when their aggression when communicating is turned toward us? There are two things to consider that will allow you to sleep through the night. The first is that their aggressiveness says more about them than you. Too many people with behaviour like this are often not aware of the damage it causes, and how hurt others can actually feel. The second is demonstrated in this story:

> *My Grandfather, Poppa-Ud, was a true saint. I remember him telling me one day how he was driving Meals on Wheels to some elderly folks, and he had to double park on the street just for two minutes. Sure enough, a man behind him really gave him the blows. He was yelling, yelling, and yelling! Poppa-Ud's response, if you can imagine, in the most accepting tone of voice: "Gee, you must be frustrated not being able to get by. I'll move right away. Hey, I bet you could use a coffee. Can I buy you one?"*

Whenever I come across a person like this, I am reminded of my Poppa-Ud and his ability to truly believe everyone has value, every minute of his or her life. This is what allowed him the respect of many throughout all his years. He was a true role model of grace.

The Value of Choosing to Influence With Wisdom: Choosing to influence with wisdom means believing that we are all equal human beings, and we are all trying to figure out life together. It means taking time for a mature approach. Know you have the right to say what you want to say, as long as it is not at the expense of others. This is easy to do, and, it is easy not to do. The payoff? *Influencing with wisdom* consistently will gain you respect, and you will also feel good about yourself. In turn, you will reach out to others even more. You get to decide your character. You get to decide if you will be a responsible communicator. You get to decide if you will honour others. And, in turn, it will be others who will determine that you influenced them with your wisdom.

Biography for Valerie Cade Lee CSP

Business Name: The Performance Curve
International
Address: Suite 356 - 100,
1039 - 17th Ave. S.W.
Calgary, Alberta T2T 0B2
Telephone: (403) 508-0678
Fax: (403) 240-9092
Email: val@performancecurve.com
Web Address: www.performancecurve.com

Canadian Association of Professional Speakers:
Calgary, Professional Member *CAPS National President, 2002*

About Valerie:

Valerie Cade Lee is an authority on Relationship Leadership. As CEO of one of Canada's largest training companies, and the 2002 National President of the Canadian Association of Professional Speakers (CAPS), Valerie demonstrates both ability and understanding.

As an accomplished professional speaker, she was one of the first women in Canada to earn the certified speaking professional designation (CSP), which is the highest earned speaking designation worldwide.

Currently, Valerie is featured on the 'Health and Science Television Network' in the US as an authority on Relationship Leadership. Her clients include top corporations in Canada, the United States, Russia, and the U.K. such as Edo Japan, Royal Bank, Canadian Payroll Association, Hitachi, and a long list of associations worldwide.

Products by Valerie:
Training CD Sets:

- *'Win / Win Assertiveness - How To Get What You Want Not at the Expense of Yourself or Others'*

- *'How To Manage Your Boss - Without Them Knowing It'*

- *'Simply World Class Professional Speaking'*

Biography for Adele Alfano

<table>
<tr><td>**Business Name:**</td><td>Diamond Within Resources: Professional Speaking and Consulting</td></tr>
<tr><td>**Address:**</td><td>75 Barlake Ave., Ste. 611, Stoney Creek, ON L8E 1G8</td></tr>
<tr><td>**Telephone:**</td><td>(905) 578-6687</td></tr>
<tr><td>**Fax:**</td><td>(905) 385-2912</td></tr>
<tr><td>**Email:**</td><td>adele@diamondwithin.com</td></tr>
<tr><td>**Web Address:**</td><td>www.diamondwithin.com</td></tr>
</table>

Canadian Association of Professional Speakers:
Hamilton, Professional member

About Adele:

WHEN DID YOU FORGET THAT YOU SPARKLE: Adele Alfano is Canada's Diamond Coach. She specializes in helping people to mine passion and purpose in their lives by exploring, discovering, and excavating their gems of self-esteem, self-acceptance, and self-worth. Her keynote and seminar topics include: 'Discovering Your Diamonds Within', and 'The Jewels of Change - Mining Treasures in an Evolving Workplace.'

Adele's presentations are described as valuable, inspiring, touching and informative. Her expertise as a 'diamond miner' makes her a popular choice by many audiences including associations and corporations. In 1998, she was nominated for 'Woman of the Year' in Hamilton.

Adele is the Past President and founding member of the Hamilton Chapter of the Canadian Association of Professional Speakers. She has worked as a certified aerobics instructor and columnist with CANWEST Communications. Today, clients include St. Joseph's Hopsital, YWCA of Canada and McMaster University enjoy her inspiring and heart-warming presentations. Her sparkling signature stories are featured in publications such as McMaster University Alumni magazine, and on Global TV's Body and Health Show.

Books by Adele:

The Expert Women Who Speak ... Speak Out! series (Co-editor).
Vol. 1, 2002 and Vol. 2, 2003

Biography for Kathy Glover Scott, M.S.W.

Business Name: Alternative Truths
Speaking and Consulting
Address: RR#4, Ingersoll, ON N5C 3J7
Telephone: (519) 425-9060
(888) 567-2119
Fax: (519) 425-1982
Email: altruth@golden.net
Web Address: www.kathygloverscott.com

Canadian Association of Professional Speakers:
Southwestern Ontario, Professional Member

About Kathy:

She has twenty years experience in the human service field as manager, business owner, agency director and psychotherapist, and holds a Masters Degree in Social Work. Her keynote presentations and training are innovative, informative and energized – and consistently rated excellent by the corporations and associations with which she works. Her topics include 'The Successful Woman', 'Stress-Busting!', and 'The Power of Your Potential'. Her online courses on 'Esteem for Personal Excellence' (3 one- hour courses) and 'The Successful Woman' (2 one-hour courses) are hosted by www.learninglibrary.com. Visit her website for more information.

Kathy is a Reiki Grand Master/Teacher. She is passionate about leading others to integrate higher forms of energy into their daily lives. She is married to Craig and they have two school-aged children.

Books by Kathy Glover Scott:

The Successful Woman: Opening up to your Limitless Potential. 2002

The Expert Women Who Speak ... Speak Out! series (Co-editor).
Vol. 1, 2002 and Vol. 2, 2003

Esteem! A Powerful Guide to Living the Life you Desire and Deserve. 2001

Esteem – The Workbook. 1999

Notes

Notes

Notes

Expert Women Who Speak... Speak Out!
Volume 2

As the editors, we would like to thank all of the contributors to this first volume of what appears to be a rapidly growing series. Again, the amazing women who contributed to this book are:

Valerie Cade Lee CSP
Jean Ryan
Janet Christensen
Tammy Adams
Gayle Church
Audrey Pihulyk
Carole Kent
Pauline Duncan-Thrasher
Dawn Brown
Joan Kulmala
Natalie Forstbauer
Arlene Jorgensen
Terri Knox
Maureen Hagan
Penny and Vicky Vilagos

For more information on upcoming volumes,
or how to be a contributor, please contact either of the editors:

Adele Alfano (www.diamondwithin.com)
or
Kathy Glover Scott (www.kathygloverscott.com)

Please visit our website: www.expertwomenwhospeak.com